"Rachelle Starr and her ministry Scarlet Hope are *amazing*! Read this inspiring, challenging book to hear unbelievable stories of life change and to have *your* life changed."

—Vince Antonucci, pastor at Verve Church

"Scarlet Hope is a beautiful example of the gospel at work, shining light into the darkness and freeing women who are in bondage."

—Liz Curtis Higgs, director of spiritual formation, Christ Church United Methodist, Louisville, KY; bestselling author of *Bad Girls of the Bible*

"I have known Rachelle for many years and am amazed at the ways that God has ministered through her! The work that Scarlet Hope is doing is rare and desperately needed. You will be both blessed and challenged at what God is doing as you read her inspiring story."

—Brian Howard, executive director, Acts 29

"You may never have Bible studies with prostitutes, but you will be invigorated and galvanized by Rachelle's infectious stories and plain-spoken truth."

—Kyle Idleman, bestselling author of *Not a Fan* and *One at a Time*

"Fifteen years ago, God called Rachelle Starr to reach women in adult entertainment for Jesus. He's used her ministry to bring so many from darkness to light. Pick up *Outrageous Obedience*, and you'll be inspired. The same faithful God at work in her is calling you to risk-taking faith."

—Jared Kennedy, editor at The Gospel Coalition, author of *The Beginner's Gospel Story Bible* and *K*---- *Your C*

"Who else would go into strip clubs and ask to provide home-cooked meals? Rachelle's ministry advances the gospel message of the saving love of Jesus Christ in a magnificent way! Only in heaven will we know the full story of how the Lord is using this work right here in my town. Amazing!"

—Mary K. Mohler, director of Seminary Wives
Institute at Southern Seminary

"Someone said God's love language is obedience. If you truly want to grow in following him, then read on. Rachelle Starr gives you a peek into her personal tug-of-war with God and her journey in obeying and following his will. Her amazing stories on these pages will inspire *you* just as her life has inspired *me*."

—Dave Stone, former senior pastor, Southeast
Christian Church, Louisville, KY

"*Outrageous Obedience* is captivating and convicting! If you're a Christian longing to see how God can work through you, Rachelle's story offers direction and encouragement. Her tale of bringing the gospel to women in the sex industry is gritty and beautiful—we can learn much about godly obedience from the lessons she's lived."

—Sarah Eekhoff Zylstra, senior writer
at The Gospel Coalition

OUTRAGEOUS
OBEDIENCE

OUTRAGEOUS OBEDIENCE

*Answering God's Call to Shine
in the Darkest Places*

RACHELLE STARR

BETHANYHOUSE

a division of Baker Publishing Group
Minneapolis, Minnesota

© 2022 by Rachelle Starr

Published by Bethany House Publishers
11400 Hampshire Avenue South
Minneapolis, Minnesota 55438
www.bethanyhouse.com

Bethany House Publishers is a division of
Baker Publishing Group, Grand Rapids, Michigan

Printed in the United States of America

ISBN 978-0-7642-4036-2 (paperback)
ISBN 978-0-7642-4125-3 (casebound)
ISBN 978-1-4934-3788-7 (ebook)
Library of Congress Cataloging-in-Publication Control Number: 2022022242

Some names and details have been changed to protect the privacy of the individuals involved.

Cover design by Emily Weigel

The author is represented by the literary agency The Gates Group, www.the-gates-group.com.

To the man who follows, acts, and trusts Jesus
to lead and love beyond himself.
Joshua, my love, none of this would be possible
without your dedication to the gospel
and sacrificial love both for me
and our family.
I love you.

CONTENTS

1

Learning to Go

There's a joke that a father's one responsibility is to keep his daughter out of a strip club. But my dad led me into them.

It all goes back to a little white church and the house next door.

The church had fourteen steps up to the entrance. A black iron cross hung over the portico, below the steeple. At the top of the steps, white double doors opened immediately into the sanctuary. A bright burgundy aisle carpet separated two rows of twelve oak pews surrounded by walls of varnished wood. At the front was the communion table, then the pulpit where my dad preached, and behind it the baptistry. The room could hold roughly one hundred people, but most often there were fifty or sixty in attendance on a Sunday morning.

If you peeked out a window to the right side of the church, you'd see the parsonage where my family lived. We had moved to Quapaw, Oklahoma, where my dad served as part-time pastor of Quapaw Christian Church in order to support the family while he attended Ozark Christian College. I was five at the time, so it's the first church I remember. Though he was only part-time, my dad served as the only pastor—with both youth and senior pastor responsibilities. My mom organized potluck meals after Sunday church. There was rarely a day when my family wasn't doing something at the church or having someone in our home for dinner.

I will never forget one of those meals. My dad brought home a kid named Steven who had been abandoned by his parents. Dad found thirteen-year-old Steven sitting in an old-fashioned phone booth at the only gas station in our small town. He had suffered at the hands of his alcoholic father, who had left him in an abandoned house to fend for himself. My dad was curious as to why he was hanging out at the filling station. Steven told him, "My only way to provide for myself is to sell drugs or beg for money."

Dad took Steven back to the abandoned house where he was living. When my father saw that it was full of trash and filth, it broke his heart. Dad couldn't let him stay there. So over dinner that night, Dad told Steven, "If you will leave your life of drugs and go back to school, you can live with us as long as you need." Steven gave up all he had known and made us his new family. My dad converted the parsonage garage into a bedroom, and Steven lived with us until he graduated from high school.

Steven longed to be loved. I can say with confidence that this was the first time in his life he felt cared for, accepted, and safe. He would come to call my parents Mom and Dad and think of my brother and me as siblings. After he graduated from high school, Steven got married and had a family of his own. I'm not sure if any of that would have happened if my dad had passed him by that day. My father's actions changed Steven's life . . . and mine.

When Dad brought Steven home, I was young, and my view of Jesus was still forming. Dad's example brought the Savior's mission to life for me. Jesus came for the sinners, the sick and dying, the outcasts and tax collectors, the thieves, murderers, and adulterers, the disabled, and the prostitutes. The Bible tells how Jesus was close to the brokenhearted, how he cared for the least of these and helped those who struggled to help themselves.

For my dad, the biblical accounts about the Savior were more than just stories. Jesus modeled the way we should live our lives today. We were to live in absolute—and what some might consider outrageous—obedience to the example Jesus set and the way he called us to live. Therefore, my dad believed our churches and homes should be filled with the people Jesus came to seek and save—the lost.

> Dad's example brought the Savior's mission to life for me. Jesus came for the sinners, the sick and dying, the outcasts and tax collectors, the thieves, murderers, and adulterers, the disabled, and the prostitutes.

One evening, we heard a knock on our parsonage door. A man who introduced himself as Alfred asked for a shower and a place to sleep that night. Alfred had been diagnosed with HIV, and he was walking across America—yes, walking the entire country, because he wanted to do something extraordinary and see new places before the virus took his life. My parents let him shower, eat dinner with us, and sleep in the church basement since our little house was full. The next day, Alfred loaded up his things and left for the next city along his journey. That encounter sparked a desire in me to be available to God whenever he put people in my path.

You see, that little town with one stop sign was where I gave my heart and life to Jesus. I sat at the Dairy Queen and told my dad, "I am a sinner. I have messed up, and I need Jesus's forgiveness. I want to give my life to him." The very next Sunday I was baptized at the little white church with the iron cross. I came out of the water to a roomful of smiling faces, many belonging to people who were a lot like Steven and Alfred. At that point in my life, I had no way of knowing how much that place and those people would affect my faith.

The Temptation to Sit Still

Later, in my early twenties, my still-new husband and I moved to a suburb of Louisville, Kentucky, in Southern Indiana. Josh had taken a job at a great local church, using his web design background to serve the kingdom.

Our lives had begun to revolve around our local church. In fact, our apartment was located across the street.

In one sense, this was a familiar life to me. We now lived as close to the church where my husband worked as my family once had lived to the little white church where my dad served as pastor. But in another sense, there were miles of difference between life in that suburban church and what

I had experienced in childhood. Everyone who attended appeared so put together. I looked around and couldn't find any people who seemed lost or needy.

I grew up with my dad bringing into church the homeless, the town drunk, people who didn't smell good or stay awake. But then as I got older and began my own journey into the first church my husband and I were members of after being married, I would look around and wonder: Where were the homeless, the broken, the people who thought the walls would implode if they walked inside? Everyone I was around had grown up in the church or was a Christian; there were very few people who didn't look like me or smell like me in this church. I began to question how I was to be used in the church to bring in the sick and the hurting. I felt dissonance between my experience there and the string of stories I knew from childhood. In this suburban church of my young adulthood, I didn't see friends bringing the hurting to Christ. Honestly, I wasn't participating in God's mission myself. My obedience to his commission was definitely less than outrageous.

Do you know that feeling? Are you at that place? If so, have you thought about what's holding you back? Have you prayed about what's kept you from moving forward?

It might be that you've gotten comfortable. God has called us to go, but it's easy to sit. To say, "I'm too busy right now. Maybe later." To sit in a church pew week after week after passing that homeless woman on the corner for the hundredth time. Trust me, I know how tempting it is to sit and to settle. But God is calling us out of our comfort and into a risk-taking partnership with him. He wants us to join him in bringing compassion and help to a hurting world.

If it's uncomfortable, it could be that you're not sure others would approve of what you believe God is calling you to do. Jesus went to the darkest places and spent time with those who were thought to be the most sinful people. He hung out with and ate meals with thieves and prostitutes in a culture where godly people were not supposed to do that. He was okay with being misunderstood and criticized, and that probably means there's something greater on the other side of obedience if we will just take the risk.

Jesus was full of compassion. He didn't focus on himself and his own needs. His compassion led him toward the hurting. He didn't wait for others to come to him. He went out to touch the untouchable with healing and hope. And he's called *us* to do the same.

God, Where Do I Go?

Whatever the reasons, I found myself in early adulthood sitting rather than going. I began to ask, "God, what am I on this earth to do? Lord, you saved me, how do you want to use me?" My asking and seeking the Lord to show me his will was the beginning of a journey to discern my calling that lasted several years. When the call finally came, it was not what I expected, but I knew without a doubt my whole life had set me up for this: *God was moving me to go and share the hope of Jesus with women in the sex industry.*

Looking back, I can see that my experiences in the little white church and the parsonage next door are what ultimately led me to this ministry. My dad modeled for me how Jesus was always surrounded by sinful people who needed his grace, and how we, as his followers, should be as well.

I was, and I am still, amazed that God called a sinner like me to join him in his work. I'm amazed that he called me to shine his light in such a dark place.

I wonder how God has called you.

I don't know, but it wouldn't surprise me if God's call on your life involves something that seems too big, too dangerous, and too much. If you're feeling led to something that will take risky faith and radical obedience, that's probably God.

Over the past decade, I have not only had the opportunity to go to women in the industry and see them saved and discipled, but I've also had the opportunity to urge, inspire, and compel others to find their calling and to be outrageously obedient.

A young woman approached me after I spoke at a conference. She had brown hair, a maroon sweater, and a bewildered look in her eyes. She said, "I've felt God put it on my heart to love people who are not like me, but it didn't make sense until now. It never dawned on me that I needed to *go to them*. I'm not even sure I can do that."

> It wouldn't surprise me if God's call on your life involves something that seems too big, too dangerous, and too much.

Another woman stood behind her anxiously waiting to chat. She seemed hopeful but nervous when she asked, "I'm in my fifties; I wish I had done what you did when I was in my twenties. Do you think it's too late for me to be used by God?"

There are also countless women who have told me, "Rachelle, the women you talked about. That was me. I may not have worked in a club, but I was lost and helpless just like them. How can I be a part of what God is doing to help other women?"

Talking with those ladies and hearing their questions helped me realize there are many women who have Christ's heart of compassion. They want to see people as Jesus sees them. They desire to shine his light in dark places and to love the unlovely. Some of these women lack the courage to say no to fear and yes to all God has for them. A few need someone who's been there to point the way—a model like my dad was for me.

I wonder if you can relate. Do you want to give your life in outrageous obedience to God's call and Jesus's mission? Do you need a friend to inspire you to be brave? Do you need direction, maybe a clear picture of where to begin?

My hope is that I can be that friend and that the stories I tell in this book will provide the imagination you need. I hope it will give you permission and direction, and that you'll learn both from how I've followed Christ and from my mistakes.

As I write this, I'm praying you will:

- See that obedience to God's call is rooted in a relationship with him.
- Know that it's his faithfulness that fuels our mission.
- Be inspired, encouraged, and equipped to put your faith into action.

That's where we're going to travel together in the pages to come. Along the way, I'm going to tell you some crazy stories. We are definitely going to laugh, we may cry a few tears, and you are going to see how loved you are and how much love you have to share.

I believe God is calling you to make a difference for him. No matter where you are—whether young or old, whether you're new to Christ or have known him for many years, whatever your background or current season of life may be. Girl, I want you to hear the Lord's call on your life and be unleashed to go be salt and light.

Wherever God is calling you, whether that be to a strip club, a homeless shelter, a pregnancy center, a mission field overseas, your church, your place of work, your neighborhood, or your home, my heart is that you'll experience eternal hope in Jesus through the pages of this book, that you will rise up to outrageous obedience, and that his light will begin to shine through you for the world to see.

PART 1

THE RELATIONSHIP DRIVES OBEDIENCE

2

Under the Black Lights

Following Jesus into the Dark

W e're hiring pretty girls, not ugly ones."
That's what the Fantasy X club sign said.
We pulled up to the large white building with blacked-out windows and parked in the front lot below the flashing pink and purple lights. I was excited but also nervous. What was I doing here? Had I lost my mind? My friend Sarah and I said a quick prayer, got out of the car, and walked up to the door.

Once in the building, we entered a long, dark hallway with a low ceiling and no windows. Posters of naked women lined the walls. At the end of the corridor, we paid a ten-dollar cover charge. This was my first time in a strip club, and I had heard that you may have to pay a cover charge to get in. I would have paid a hundred dollars if it gave me the chance to talk to the women working there.

We stepped inside the lounge. It felt like we'd gone back in time. Nothing had been updated since the place opened in the seventies. Decades of nicotine clung to the walls, and the thick, stale smoke made it hard to breathe. The blaring music and fogged light from a few bare lightbulbs also made it difficult to hear and see. And the smell? It was a combination of stale sweat, moldy carpet, and layers of grime on every surface.

Although I had never been to a strip club before, as I looked around this world I didn't know, I felt in my spirit that it was precisely where God wanted me to be. Before walking in, I had visualized scary people, but that is not what we saw. Under those harsh lights, we looked into the eyes of weary women who had lost their hope and lost their way. As I stood there, I could sense their broken dreams and feelings of worthlessness. I didn't want that for these women. I looked at them, and I instead saw daughters of the King.

We stepped up to the bar, and the bartender seemed puzzled. I guess we didn't look like the normal clientele. She asked us, "What brings you here tonight?"

"Are you the manager?" I asked.

"No. What do you want?"

Exploitation in America

Fantasy X is one of nearly four thousand sexually explicit businesses in the United States—and that only counts the legal establishments. Strip clubs alone account for seven billion dollars of adult entertainment revenue. Tens of thousands of women are exploited in these clubs every week.[1]

1. "Strip Clubs Industry in the US—Market Research Report," *IBISWorld* (industry research group), April 2, 2021, https://www.ibisworld.com/united-states/market-research-reports/strip-clubs-industry/.

How the Adult Entertainment Industry Devalues Women

- A 2008 report by the Chicago Alliance Against Sexual Exploitation found that 40 percent of sex buyers paid for sex with women they knew to be under the control of a pimp or trafficker.
- 43 percent of buyers said that if they pay for sex, the woman should do anything they ask.
- 13 percent said they would rape a woman if they knew they could get away with it; 19 percent said they have.*

*Rachel Durchslag and Samir Goswami, *Deconstructing the Demand for Prostitution: Preliminary Insights from Interviews with Chicago Men Who Purchase Sex* (Chicago Alliance Against Sexual Exploitation, 2008), https://humantraffickinghotline.org/sites/default/files /Deconstructing-the-Demand-for-Prostitution%20-%20CAASE.pdf.

Exploitation is not something that merely "happens in Vegas." It's happening in your neighborhood.

Many people think the women who dance in strip clubs do it because they want to. However, groups that work to fight sex trafficking have reported that 70 percent of females who are bought and sold in the United States are trafficked into the adult entertainment industry. They are forced into it against their will. The adult entertainment industry includes the pornography industry, massage parlors, and your local strip club.[2] The whole industry devalues women. It strips them not only of their clothes but of their dignity. Consider the statistics in the sidebar.

Such statistics about sex buyers show their selfish carelessness and the ways they diminish women into commodities.

2. Stephanie Sandoval, "The Connection Between Adult Entertainment and Sex Trafficking," *Qualified* (blog), March 27, 2017, https://qualifiedwomen.com /2017/03/27/adult-entertainment-sex-trafficking/.

One man interviewed in the Chicago study said, "Prostitutes are like a product, like cereal. You go to the grocery, pick the brand you want, and pay for it. It's business."[3] For the traffickers, exploiting women is simply a profitable business. Pimps regularly withhold pay from, threaten, and physically abuse their victims. They also sometimes induce women into using addictive drugs, which gives them another level of control.[4] All the while, the pimps become wealthy. A 2016 report said pimps in the San Diego area averaged $670,625 in annual income.[5]

Strip clubs are equally profitable, and their treatment of exotic dancers is nearly as oppressive as the treatment of women on the street corners. According to a 2004 article:[6]

- 23 percent of the dancers that were surveyed reported having been forced to have sex.
- 51 percent reported being threatened with a weapon.
- 48 percent had been threatened with rape.

It's dark and scary under the black lights.

3. Durchslag and Goswami, *Deconstructing the Demand*, 16.
4. Kyleigh Feehs and Alyssa Currier Wheeler, *2020 Federal Human Trafficking Report* (Human Trafficking Institute, 2021), https://traffickinginstitute.org/wp-content/uploads/2022/01/2020-Federal-Human-Trafficking-Report-Low-Res.pdf.
5. Ami Carpenter and Jamie Gates, "The Nature and Extent of Gang Involvement in Sex Trafficking in San Diego County" (San Diego: University of San Diego and Point Loma Nazarene University, 2016), a paper presented to the United States Department of Justice, https://www.ncjrs.gov/pdffiles1/nij/grants/249857.pdf/.
6. Jody Raphael and Deborah L. Shapiro, "Violence in Indoor and Outdoor Prostitution Venues," *Violence Against Women* 10, no. 2 (February 2004): 126–39, https://doi.org/10.1177/1077801203260529.

Love Shows Up

Stories and statistics from human trafficking and the adult entertainment industry should stir our hearts and move us to go and shine God's light in dark places. Fantasy X's presence certainly moved the church people in my city to action. Christians were not blind to what was happening at Fantasy X. They saw it as a problem, and they tried to shut the club down.

How? By calling the police, showing up at city council meetings, and picketing on the sidewalk. Church people posted pictures of license plates in the parking lot, seeking to embarrass the men who went in as patrons. A local faith-based newspaper even ran a series on the evils of places like Fantasy X. Everything they wrote was true.

But was it effective? I've never yet seen shame change a life.

I wonder how you would view the Fantasy X club. Would you even notice it? If you did, would you feel condemnation or compassion for the people inside? The Bible says of Jesus, "When he saw the crowds, he had compassion for them, because they were harassed and helpless, like sheep without a shepherd" (Matthew 9:36 ESV). Would you feel that way, or would you feel like they've made their choices and deserve whatever they get? And if you did want to do something about what was happening in the clubs, what would you do?

I looked at Fantasy X differently from the church people in my city. Every weekday for more than a year, I passed that club on my way to work. As I drove past, I kept thinking about what God was asking of me. I called out to him, and I asked

for eyes to see what he wanted me to see. I saw the sign—
pretty girls, not ugly ones—and I thought, *Every girl is made in
God's image.* I wasn't thinking about the activity that went on
inside that club. What God put on my heart was the people—
the women who gave lap dances to patrons, the servers sell-
ing drinks, the dancers who had to take their clothes off in
front of everyone, and even the owners counting the money.

My heart broke for the people trapped inside the strip
clubs throughout my city. They were like sheep without a
shepherd. I longed for a way to reach the women and men
inside those walls. Picketing, shouting insults, and shutting
down the clubs would not change these women. Activism
would not save them. Only Jesus could do that. Christians
were trying to raise awareness about *the evils of adult entertainment*, but I believe it was just raising barriers between
them and the *people* in adult entertainment. I believe Jesus
was calling me to go and bring his hope to the people in the
club. To follow him felt exciting . . . scary . . . outrageous,
but I wanted to obey no matter how difficult it might be.

When I considered meeting women in the clubs, I
thought about one of Jesus's disciples—Matthew. When
Jesus called him, Matthew was sitting at a tax collector's
booth. Collecting revenue for Rome was one of the most
despised occupations during Jesus's time. The Jewish people
would have considered Matthew to be a traitor, working for
the oppressive and tyrannical Roman government, doing
Caesar's bidding. Matthew may have also been a swindler,
making extra money by taking advantage of the poor. But
Jesus still called Matthew as one of his first followers.

When Matthew said yes, he immediately threw a party,
to which he invited all his sinful associates . . . and Jesus.

Jesus accepted the invitation and happily went into what the holier-than-thou crowd would have considered the heart of darkness.

When the religious leaders saw Jesus associating with Matthew the tax collector and his sinful friends, they were taken aback and asked, "Why does your teacher eat with tax collectors and sinners?" But upon hearing this, Jesus replied, "It is not the healthy who need a doctor, but the sick. . . . I have not come to call the righteous, but sinners" (Matthew 9:11–13). That's what Jesus does. He calls the guilty and reaches out to the marginalized.

Jesus's invitation transformed Matthew from the inside out. That same Matthew became the author of the first Gospel, a book that unpacks the most important happenings of Jesus's ministry. The despised traitor wrote a portion of Scripture! And God used Matthew's Gospel in my own life to shape my love for Jesus and to put a burning desire in my heart to live like him.

Love Takes Action

On that first night, my friend Sarah and I purposefully wore plain black turtlenecks and no makeup. We wanted to make sure none of the patrons hit on us. And we didn't know if the owners would consider us pretty or ugly, but either way, we wanted them to know we weren't there for a job. We clearly looked out of place.

"What do you want?" the bartender asked us curtly. She didn't know what to think of us. I'm sure my response caught her even more off guard: "Jesus sent us here to do something kind and loving for the women in this club. Could we maybe bring in a home-cooked meal?"

Ever since, that simple line has often opened doors for us to serve women in local clubs. It's even led to our being able to share the gospel of hope in Christ. But that first night when I uttered those words, the bartender's eyes just stared back vacantly.

"*Well*," she said, "we already have food, but thanks anyway."

In Kentucky at the time, alcohol and nude dancing weren't allowed in the same room. So this club was divided in half. Partially clothed dancers served drinks at a bar on one side. On the other side, nude dancers performed, and patrons were served Coke, pretzels, and candy. A makeshift sex paraphernalia shop was right in between.

We didn't want to give up after our initial conversation with the bartender, so we walked through the shop to the other side to look for a manager. When our eyes finally got accustomed to the dark, we made our way to a high-top table where we tried to look comfortable. (It took Academy Award–level acting!) Then, we just waited there for God to tell us what to do.

Dancers passed by and asked if we wanted a drink or a lap dance. I quickly told one of the ladies we weren't interested, and instead asked how her day was going. As we stood eye to eye, she looked so sad. Each woman who approached seemed puzzled and quickly headed in another direction.

The few minutes we waited seemed like forever. Then, I felt the Spirit prompt me to talk to one guy in a crowd of about thirty men. He was young, tall, and blond. I could not understand why the Spirit led me to talk to this particular man. As I made my way to his table, I had no idea what I was going to say to him. I approached and stuck out my hand.

"Hi, my name is Rachelle, I'm not here for a job," (as if the turtleneck didn't make that clear), "but I am here because Jesus sent me. We want to do something kind and loving for the women in this place. Can we bring in a home-cooked meal to the ladies?"

He looked suspicious and asked, "What's the catch?"

"There is no catch," I exclaimed. "I'm just here with my friend to show the love of Christ to the women who work here."

For the next forty-five minutes, I talked with this young man, who turned out to be the owner of the club. How cool is it that God led me to the right person! It might sound crazy, but I've found when we take blind steps of faith, our all-seeing God—who knows it all—will meet us in the unknown. That's what takes fear out of faith. Not trusting in our limited capabilities but trusting in God's unlimited care.

Alan was in his early twenties and built like a tall bouncer. I smiled and, not yet knowing he was the owner, asked, "How long have you been working here?"

"I've only ever known the clubs," Alan explained. "My parents owned the place. I remember celebrating my seventh birthday here with a lap dance."

I don't think he told me that for shock value. He seemed serious. As Alan grew up, his parents told him they would one day hand him the keys to the club and let him run the place. So here he was.

Alan also shared his experience with Christians. His only encounters were with a church in the area that had tried to shut the place down. Thankfully, we weren't from that church, or his welcome wouldn't have lasted long.

"Well, I don't know about them," I said, "but my church would welcome you—and any women from here." It would be a long time before I could share the gospel with Alan, but that conversation was a first step in helping him see that forgiveness and redemption are for him too.

That's another lesson I've learned along the way—even if we're not preaching it yet, we're always planting seeds of the gospel. That means every conversation is an opportunity; it may be a step on the journey of someone saying yes to Jesus.

Intrigued with the idea of "church ladies" bringing a meal into his club, Alan asked when we could come back. Working hard to keep my eyes from popping out of my head, I shot back, "How about Thursday? We'll bring our first meal Thursday at 8:30 p.m. on the dot."

"See ya then!" Alan answered.

Shocked and ecstatic, Sarah and I headed out of the club and met up with our drivers—our husbands—who were anxiously waiting in the parking lot. We shouted with joy about what the Lord had just done. He'd opened a door that only he could open.

Love Comes to Dinner

What's the most memorable meal you've ever made?

Several come to mind for me. Last year I hosted my family for Thanksgiving for the first time. I spent a week planning and preparing. I also think back to when I was doing private catering. One time I was in the middle of giving a grandiose demonstration when I turned around to get the thermometer out of a pork tenderloin. I grabbed the 400-degree thermometer . . . with my bare hand! And I started screaming like a teenager being chased by a killer in a horror movie. Not my best moment.

I love how just after Matthew had his all-time best moment—when he was called by Jesus—he threw a dinner party. We don't know what he made for the meal, but we do know who he invited. "While Jesus was having dinner at Matthew's house, many tax collectors and sinners came and ate with him and his disciples" (Matthew 9:10). Think about it. There they were—Jesus, Matthew, *and the sinners*—breaking bread, reclining around the table, sharing a meal.

That table is a perfect picture for me of what eternity is going to be like. It will be a place where sinners like me and tax collectors and prostitutes will all feast at a table together with Jesus himself. Why? Because Jesus came to seek and save the lost. Each one of us is lost before Christ. We are blind until he opens our eyes to see how he paid for our sins upon the cross. We are hopeless until his love shows up and invites us to the table.

Through the middle of that week, Sarah and I planned the meal we would take on Thursday. I was so excited I could hardly sleep. I'm an Italian girl who learned to cook from Mom and Nonna back in New York, so I baked a hearty, million-dollar spaghetti filled with mozzarella, hamburger meat, sausage, and marinara. Sarah prepared a salad, and together we baked delicious garlic bread, cookies, and brownies.

We arrived back at the club that Thursday at 8:30 p.m.—just as promised—and carried in all the food with the serving ware. We asked where to set it up. The DJ, a guy named Jimmy, heard we were coming, so he was ready with a white pop-up table right in front of his booth. I was so relieved Alan hadn't forgotten about us.

As we put out the spread, all eyes in the room were on us. Sarah stayed at the table, and I walked around to some of the women who were sitting by themselves, trying to invite them to have dinner.

The first woman looked at me and said flatly, "No, thanks. I already ate."

A second woman asked, "How much does it cost?"

"Nothing," I responded. "It's free."

She tentatively made her way over to the table, and we began to make her a plate. Then I introduced myself. "Hi, I'm Rachelle, and this is Sarah. What's your name?"

"Nice to meet you." She smiled. "I'm Ashley. So, what catering business are y'all from?" She had to be thinking, *What kind of catering business gives away free meals in a strip club?*

I chuckled a little. "We aren't from a catering company." I said a quick prayer before explaining, "We're bringing food because Jesus loves you, and he wanted us to tell you that tonight."

"Well, no one has ever done *that* before," said Ashley, puzzled. She couldn't believe someone would offer her food for free and, I think, couldn't figure out what Jesus had to do with it.

Only one woman ate. The others stared at us, wondering why we were *really* there. It felt a little awkward—okay, it felt a lot awkward. It wasn't what we had hoped for, but it was okay. If you try something great for God, it might start small, and that's okay. I love the reassurance we get in Zechariah 4:10 (NLT), "Do not despise these small beginnings, for the LORD rejoices to see the work begin."

As we showed up, week after week, bringing meals and compassionate listening ears, we earned their trust. And one by one we got to know the women. We heard about their lives—their kids and hobbies. And about the way they viewed Christians before we walked in. Jesus taught us—little by little, moment by moment—to listen to them and to his Spirit. As we obeyed his promptings, he did the rest. He'd show up time and time again, giving us words to say.

Sometimes people in the church can think the way Jesus loved—the way he moved toward sinners and touched the despised—is the kind of ministry meant for someone else. We rejoice in what Jesus did for us, but we don't see how he calls us to do the same. Shane Claiborne describes it this way:

> We can admire and worship Jesus without doing what he did. We can applaud what he preached and stood for without caring about the same things. We can adore his cross without taking up ours.[7]

Could you go back and read that quote one more time? How does it make you feel? Guilty? Inspired?

I read that quote from Claiborne before God called me to reach out to women in the adult entertainment industry; it had a profound impact on my life. I didn't want to think

7. Shane Claiborne, *The Irresistible Revolution: Living as an Ordinary Radical* (New York: Harper Collins, 2006), 113.

that what Jesus said or did was for someone else. The truth is that what Jesus has done for us *as* sinners should move us to do the same *for* sinners. We move toward them, touch them, and meet their needs.

I read that quote and it broke me. It convicted me out of my complacency. I desperately wanted to love people with the same sacrificial kindness and love with which Jesus first loved me.

That's what Jesus asks of us. He didn't invite us just to believe in him. He said, "Follow me." We're to live like he lived and do what he did. Jesus went to the darkest places and to the people most enmeshed in sin. I decided I would follow him into the darkness of a strip club—under the black lights—to shine his light by putting his love into action.

Make no mistake, this book isn't about me or how brave I am. Instead, this is a story about our amazing God, who gives courage to those who are willing to follow Jesus into the dark places to rescue his children whom he loves. He's calling you to do that. And I want to assure you: when you say yes to his call, he will make you brave.

> To be clear, this book is not about strip-club ministry—it's about you being obedient to whatever call God has put on your life.

This book also isn't about you going into strip clubs. Many of my stories are from that world because that's where God has sent me. But to be clear, this book is not about strip-club ministry—it's about you being obedient to whatever call God has put on your life.

Outrageous obedience to God's call is rooted in a relationship with Jesus. His faithfulness fuels our mission. With his Spirit, we learn to take risks, overcome fear, and bring others along as we go. As we follow Jesus, we become salt and light in a dark world.

Throughout this book, you'll discover the key to following Jesus into the dark is loving people one at a time—and continuing to love them no matter how they respond. That may involve loving a person who spits in your face, someone who mocks Jesus, or the nasty neighbor who refuses to say hello. We show up. We act in love. Then we show up again. And again. And act in love again. And again. Until we finally break through their barriers.

You might wonder if you're capable of loving like that. I understand. I've had those same doubts. Good news: We don't manufacture love for others. We receive love from God, and then we have love to give. "We love because he first loved us" (1 John 4:19). So you may not have the kind of love you need within you, but you have a God who loves you with a ridiculous, unconditional, audacious, overwhelming love. God pours his love into our hearts through his Holy Spirit (Romans 5:5), and then we have love, *his love*, to give.

You have a God who loves you with a ridiculous, unconditional, audacious, overwhelming love.

God is calling you to follow Jesus into the unknown. He's calling you to go. But you're about to see that it's not just that God is calling you. Your entire life, he's been pursuing and preparing you for your calling.

3

By My Bedside

Meeting Jesus in Your Pain

What's the most painful thing you've ever been through?

If you think back through your life, what memories of suffering come to your mind? Perhaps you . . .

- grew up without a mom or dad
- were sexually abused in some way, like so many of the women trapped in the adult entertainment industry
- had a husband who wasn't true to his vows and then were dragged through a divorce
- know the unique agony of having a prodigal child

Think about how you felt in the middle of that hurt. Do you remember what question you were asking? For many, the question is *Why?* As in, *Why did this happen? Why do I have to go through it? Why doesn't God prevent it and protect me?*

I believe there's a better question: *What?*

The Spot

I was three years old when my parents noticed the spot on my back.

During my toddler years, Dad was a Bible college student at a small school in the Ozark Mountains. My parents were young, and they didn't have much, so during Dad's first year of college we lived with my grandparents at their home in the country. My grandfather worked as a general contractor, and my grandparents' property included a few acres, a big barn with a wood shop, several cats, and some big dog pens where they kept their Dobermans. My brother and I loved to play hide-and-seek in the barn and out in the fields. When the dogs were out, I'd even hide from my brother by climbing up inside the huge doghouses.

We were outside all the time. So when my parents saw that spot and called my aunt, who is a nurse, she took one look and said, "The girl's picked up ringworm out in the doghouses. She needs to get that checked out."

Ringworm? Every girl's dream!

Honestly, I don't really remember that first doctor's visit. Mom tells me the physician gave us an anti-fungal cream to put on the red patch, but it didn't help. The ring in my skin kept growing.

Two years later, around the time I turned five, I'd been to dozens of doctors—dermatologists at first, then infectious disease specialists. By that point, I was just getting sicker and sicker. My hands and feet began to stiffen, and the skin on my back, legs, and arms was hardening.

Finally, my parents took me to a children's hospital where I was diagnosed with *scleroderma*. That is a condition you may have only heard about on episodes of *House* or *Grey's Anatomy*. Scleroderma is caused by an abundance of collagen in a person's body that attacks their immune system. The form of scleroderma I had—what was called *morphea* at the time—causes patches of reddish skin on a person's abdomen, back, appendages, and sometimes even on their face. The patches, formed by the hardened collagen in the skin, thicken into firm, oval-shaped areas. That's what I'd been experiencing for the previous two years.

My primary doctor and the other physicians there were concerned that the hardened collagen in my skin might spread to my internal organs. So they brought me in to have all sorts of tests done—on my esophagus, liver, lungs . . . on what felt like my entire body.

There were a few things that complicated my case of scleroderma:

First, when the doctors diagnosed me, there were only ten other cases of children in the United States with scleroderma; more often the disease had been seen in women aged fifty and older. The doctors couldn't understand why it was affecting me.

Second, I had a related condition called *Raynaud's phenomenon*. It's a problem caused by blood vessels in your hands that spasm and cause decreased blood flow to your fingers. The spasms occur in response to cold, stress, or feeling emotionally upset. That's what was causing my hands and feet to seize up.

Third, there was no medicine available at the time to treat the illness directly. I was put on steroids to help my immune response. I went to daily, painful physical therapy sessions. The goal was to keep me mobile, to help me learn to open and stretch out my stiffened limbs, hands, fingers, and feet. Beginning at age five, I slept every night wearing hand splints.

Red patches *and* hand splints? Yes, I was the envy of every girl in my class.

My favorite pair were made from pink casts with purple Velcro around them. The splints attached around my arms and fit tightly to my hands. Mom would stretch my fingers open and put them in the pink casts each night. It was painful. There was a long season of my childhood when I can remember asking, "Am I going to be like this forever?"

Called from Suffering

My parents would probably tell you that nothing in life really bothers me. I'm the kind of girl who just keeps going. But as I went through the doctors' visits, tests, and therapy with red patches on my skin and splints on my hands, I often felt worthless and hopeless. Sometimes after difficult days, I'd cry myself to sleep.

The question I was struggling with during that time was *Why?*

I've since learned the better question is *What?* As in, *What is God's plan to use this in my life? What does God want me to do? What can I do to live out my purpose in this?* We all go through pain and suffering. Jesus tells us in John 16:33 that we will have trouble, but to take heart because he has overcome the world. So, if we are promised pain and suffering, we should begin to ask the Holy Spirit, "What do you want me to do with this?"

You've heard, "God never wastes a hurt," and "God can turn your misery into your ministry." Those phrases are trite. They're also true.

The people God calls to minister to the hurting have often been hurt themselves. They've experienced deep trauma and pain. They've suffered, been weak, and perhaps been despised, and it has given them a heart for people going through trauma and pain. They've become the sort of people who can comfort others. Why? Because they've first received comfort themselves (1 Corinthians 1:28; 2 Corinthians 1:4).

> You've heard, "God never wastes a hurt," and "God can turn your misery into your ministry." Those phrases are trite. They're also true.

We discover that in our pain, God is preparing us for his purpose. And that struggling through intense trials allows a person to be used by God in incredibly powerful ways.

There's Something about Mary

The work God calls each of us to is vital to the kingdom. God wouldn't be calling you to it if it wasn't something he planned and purposed for you to do. But not all of our acts of obedience or callings will be in the spotlight or will be noticed. Maybe it's sitting with elderly people who do not have loved ones, it's the quiet moments that you lift up the barista at Starbucks or the cashier at the grocery. It's a note left on the desk of someone who lost a project or is overwhelmed at work. It's the call to the newly pregnant single mom who is scared to death to be a mother. These are subtle acts of obedience we are all called to. Many ordinary, hardly noticed people, especially women, were part of Jesus's ministry. But they were noticed by Jesus, and that's what is most important as we follow him.

Have you ever wondered how Jesus and the Twelve supported their itinerant ministry financially? I have! One time we see Jesus pull a coin out of the mouth of a fish and use it to pay a tax. Was that a regular thing? Were fish like Jesus's ATM machines? And did the disciples sell the nets full of fish they miraculously caught? Were they able to charge a little extra because the fish were supernaturally sourced?

We don't really know, except for a hint we get in Luke 8. Luke tells us about a time when Jesus "traveled about from one town and village to another, proclaiming the good news of the kingdom of God" (Luke 8:1). Luke explains that a group of women—Mary Magdalene, Joanna, Susanna, and others—traveled with Jesus and his companions. We're told that these women "had been cured of evil spirits and diseases" (Luke 8:2). In fact, Mary Magdalene was known as the one "from whom seven demons had come out" (Luke 8:2). And we learn that these women who traveled with Jesus—the very women who had been delivered from disease and demons—supported the Savior and his disciples "out of their own means" (Luke 8:3).

Here's a group of women who had been sick and oppressed. They'd experienced pain and trauma. (I'd call seven demons traumatic! One sounds like a lot to me; Mary had

44

seven!) Then, they met Jesus and received healing, deliverance, and divine comfort.

These same women—having been rescued from sin and brokenness—reoriented their lives for the Savior. They leveraged their *connections* (Luke tells us that Joanna was the wife of Chuza, who was the manager of Herod's household) and their *resources* (this was a group of women with means!) for the sake of Jesus's mission. As a result, the good news of the kingdom expanded throughout the towns and villages of Judea and Galilee.

God Was Up to Something

When I was struggling with scleroderma, it not only felt painful but also pointless. But now, looking back, I can see God's plan. In my pain, he was preparing me for his purpose.

During my ongoing, disheartening battle with scleroderma, my family drew near to me with healing comfort. Their example taught me how to give compassionate care to people who are trapped in painful situations and can't find a way out. That's what I do today.

My grandfather showed me special kindness and communicated to me that I was unconditionally loved. That helped me understand I was more than the sickness I was tempted to let define me. Grandpa defended and fought for me. Honestly, I don't know where I'd be without him. And it's not lost on me that today my ministry includes showing kindness and unconditional love to women who think their sin defines them; my ministry is now defending and fighting for them.

My dad was more intentional about discipling me. He led me spiritually in all kinds of ways, and there was extra time for that when I was sick. He prayed for me each night and read books to me while sitting by my bedside.

Dad trained me to know Scripture. His own bright red Bible was ragged around the edges with highlights and sections underlined with pen on every page. Dad wanted me to have that same sort of weathered relationship with God's Word. When I was ten, he had me write out the entire book of Matthew multiple times in a journal.

He also had this embarrassing old Jeep he'd take me to school in each day. There was always blue smoke billowing out of the tail pipe and index cards with memory passages littered across the front console. Dad would make me rehearse those verses with him every morning. "Tell it to me again," he'd say. Those Scripture passages (with the references!) are still locked in my brain. I draw from them nearly every day in ministering to ladies in clubs.

Dad also told me stories, especially when I was sick and stuck in bed. One evening, he sat down by my bed and told me a story that grabbed and inspired me. It was about the Christian sociologist Tony Campolo, who had flown from the east coast to Honolulu for a speaking engagement. Experiencing some jet lag, Campolo woke up at three o'clock in the morning. He was hungry and unable to get back to sleep, so he wandered into the city and found coffee and a greasy donut at a twenty-four-hour diner. Here's how Campolo tells what happened next:

> I'm drinking my coffee and eating this dirty donut when into the room came about eight or nine prostitutes. They sat down on either side of me, and I tried to disappear.

Then the one on my immediate right, said, "Tomorrow's my birthday. I'm going to be thirty-nine." Her friend said, "So what do you want me to do? Sing happy birthday? You want a cake? Should we have a party for you?"

The first woman said, "Look, I'm not expecting anything. I just . . . Why do you have to put me down?" And then she said with a crack in her voice, "I've never had a birthday party my whole life. I don't expect to have one now."[1]

Campolo stayed at the counter until the women left. Then he called over the diner's kitchen staff, a couple named Harry and Jane. Harry told him the woman who had never had a birthday party was named Agnes. Campolo responded with an idea: "What do you say we decorate the place, and when she comes in tomorrow, we'll have a birthday party for her?" Harry said, "Mister, that's brilliant." Campolo continues the story:

So I got there the next morning about two-thirty. I had bought crepe paper at the K-mart, strung it across the place, and made a big sign that said, "Happy Birthday, Agnes!" I put it on the mirror behind the counter. I had the place spruced. Jane got the word out on the streets so that by three-fifteen every prostitute in Honolulu was squeezed into this place. . . . It was wall-to-wall prostitutes and me.

Three-thirty in the morning, the door opens and in comes Agnes and her friends. I got everybody poised. "Everybody ready?" The minute she walked through the door, we yell, "Happy Birthday, Agnes!" and all start cheering like mad. I've never seen anybody so stunned in my life.

1. Andy Gill, "Tony Campolo—Party with Prostitutes," *YouTube* (August 3, 2011), accessed online at https://www.youtube.com/watch?v=DRBM_YY_YX0.

Later on, Agnes stepped out with her birthday cake to show it to her mom, who lived two doors down from the diner. While she was gone, Campolo led the uneasy group in prayer. When he said "Amen" and lifted his eyes, Harry was standing in front of him face-to-face.

"You're no sociologist. You're a preacher. What kind of church you belong to?" It was one of those moments when you come up with just the right words. I said, "I belong to a church that throws birthday parties for whores at three-thirty in the morning."

I thought that was a clever answer. I'll never forget his response. He looked back and he said, "No, you don't. No, you don't." He said, "I would join a church like *that*."

I love that story because that *is* the kind of church Jesus came to establish. Campolo gave a gift to a woman who felt undeserving of a gift because she thought she was ugly, nasty, and unlovable. When my dad told me the story, I didn't know God would one day call me to serve broken women in the sex industry. But God knew. He was planting seeds in the soil of my sickness, seeds that would one day blossom into a ministry that can be similar to what happened in that diner in Hawaii.

Can I ask again: If you think back through your life, what memories of suffering come to your mind? What have you gone through, and what might God have been up to? I don't mean that he caused the trauma that happened in your life, but I know he can bring good out of the bad. And I believe he has a plan that includes you stepping out of your comfort zone to bring hope to the hurting and hopeless. So, what hurts has he brought you through? And what did he do in the midst of them to prepare you for his purpose?

So often our testimony comes out of our trauma and our ministry out of our misery. We each have unique things we've gone through. But one trauma we have in common is that we're all desperate sinners who could only be saved by amazing grace.

When we begin to see ourselves that way—as sick and sinful and utterly reliant on the mercy of a compassionate God—not only will we live with profound gratitude, but we will also be motivated and prepared to love and minister to broken and desperate people.

Finding Ourselves in Christ's Story

Think back to when you were a child. Maybe you loved to ride your bike, or play hide-and-seek in a barn, or chase your siblings and friends down the street. When you were told a story back then, do you remember how easy it was to imagine yourself inside it? If you have kids in your life, you see it in them. Little girls dress up like their favorite princess from the Disney movies; they want to *be* Cinderella or Rapunzel. A young boy reads about Superman in a comic book and immediately wraps a makeshift cape around his shoulders and attempts to fly.

But as we grow toward maturity, we're taught to read differently. Richard Plass and James Cofield describe it this way:

> Most of our training and practice of reading in our educational experience has been for the purpose of mastering material and increasing our knowledge. . . . We have done

this for so long that we believe reading for mastery is the only kind of reading there is.[2]

If you've been a part of a Bible study at a solid local church, you've probably learned how to use a study Bible and know the importance of understanding the historical background behind the book of the Bible you're reading. You may even know how to recognize different Bible genres, conduct a word study, and trace biblical themes across the Old and New Testaments. These are important skills, because they center us on the biblical authors' intended meaning and guard against reading our own opinions into the text.

> **If we're only reading the Bible for factual information, or even theological inspiration, we can miss the experience of communion with God and the transformation he has in store for our lives.**

But the trouble with this approach is that if we're only reading the Bible for factual information, or even theological inspiration, we can miss the experience of communion with God and the transformation he has in store for our lives. If we're only reading the Bible for mastery of the content, we fail to be *mastered by it*.

"It's possible to study the Bible without ever encountering the living God," write Plass and Cofield.

This is what happened to the Pharisees. They studied but missed the point of Scripture, which is an encounter with

2. Richard Plass and James Cofield, *The Relational Soul: Moving from False Self to Deep Connection* (Downers Grove, IL: IVP Books, 2014), 138.

Jesus (John 5:39). Without the Spirit of Christ, the Bible is not a life-giving word. The signs and symbols of words on a page have life only in that they point toward what is alive and true.[3]

I like to spend time with the Savior in the morning. I'll begin by asking the Holy Spirit to speak to me through the Word. If it's a passage I've read a hundred times, I ask him to give me new eyes to understand the Scripture in a different way. I pick one book of the Bible to work through during this devotional time, and I read through it slowly— verse by verse, paragraph by paragraph. I read until I sense what the Spirit behind the words (and never contrary to the words) is saying about the passage. Then, I write that down in my journal.

What I love to do, and find most powerful, is to imagine myself as part of the story. But unlike my childhood self, I no longer see myself in the text as the hero or princess. Instead, I now realize . . . I'm the Agnes in need of a birthday party.

Do you see yourself that way? The truth is, we're all broken, trapped in our sin and pain. But Jesus sees us. He knows our names. He loves us despite our sin. And he brings us more than a birthday party. He brings us healing and salvation. He gives us a *spiritual* birthday party, calling us into relationship with him.

When I read the Bible, I need to realize I'm the person in the story who is sick, sinful, and in need of grace.

For instance, when I read the beautiful description of the Servant of the Lord in Isaiah 61, I don't just see that

3. Plass and Cofield, *The Relational Soul*, 139.

Jesus's mission involved proclaiming good news to the poor, binding up the brokenhearted, and proclaiming freedom to the captives (Isaiah 61:1). I must recognize that *I* am one of the poor, broken, and enslaved. The Savior came to comfort me in my mourning, to give me a crown of beauty instead of ashes, and to make me an oak of righteousness, a planting of the Lord for the display of his splendor (Isaiah 61:2–3).

This is a book about being on mission with Jesus. But the truth is, that mission doesn't begin when you sign up to serve with your local church, crisis pregnancy center, or homeless shelter, or when you minister to prostitutes in a diner at three-thirty in the morning. Yes, that story helped inspire me to serve people in the sex industry like Agnes. But before that could happen, I needed to see myself *in* the story *as Agnes*. As a sinner in need of grace. It's recognizing my desperate need for grace that compels me to extend grace to others.

> **If you're going to hear God when he tells you to "Go," you've got to be familiar with his voice.**

Your call to be on mission with Jesus begins with his mission to save and rescue you. It begins when you find yourself in his story as the one who needs his comfort and healing touch.

Once we receive his grace and come into relationship with him, our call to be on mission continues as we take time to listen to the Spirit and hear him speak to us personally. After all, if you're going to hear God when he tells you to "Go," you've got to be familiar with his voice.

Recognizing His Voice When He Calls

Remember Mary Magdalene? The one whom Jesus healed of more than half a dozen demons?

The Sunday morning after the crucifixion, Mary went to Jesus's tomb (John 20). Once she arrived, she discovered the stone had been rolled away from the entrance. It was bad enough for her dear Jesus to be crucified that Friday. Now, she assumed, a thief must have taken his body.

Mary had brought spices to anoint Jesus's body; it was the first step in what would be a year-long embalming ritual. But with the body missing, she wasn't certain what she should do. So Mary just stood there outside the tomb, crying.

That's when Mary noticed others there. She didn't realize it was two angels, who asked her, "Woman, why are you crying?"

"They have taken my Lord away," she said, "and I don't know where they have put him" (John 20:13).

Mary turned, and another voice spoke to her. He asked, "'Woman, why are you crying? Who is it you are looking for?' Thinking he was the gardener, she said, 'Sir, if you have carried him away, tell me where you have put him, and I will get him.'"

Then, "Jesus said to her, 'Mary'" (John 20:15–16).

He knew her name. And Mary knew his voice. Though she thought he was dead, though her tears were still fresh, there was no mistaking that voice. This was the same voice that commanded seven evil spirits to leave her and end their oppression. This was the man she'd followed and helped to support with her own means. She'd spent time with him. This was her teacher and Lord.

"Rabboni!" Mary cried out, and then she reached for him. Mary had once been rescued by Jesus's healing touch. She now received comfort from his presence. Her grief was taken away in the face of her Savior.

Mary's story had sin, then saving. Pain, then healing. And Mary's story didn't end there.

In that moment, Mary was filled with relief and joy. She reached out to Jesus. She wanted to be near him. She wanted to sink into the comfort of his presence. She wanted to *stay*. Jesus told her no. Not yet. Then he gave her a command: "Go."

That voice she had come to know and love told her, "*Go* and tell them!" Jesus called her to be the first witness to his resurrection. And do you know what Mary did? She obeyed that voice and stepped into her calling. Immediately, Mary rose to GO.

Your story has sin, then saving. Pain, then healing. And your story doesn't end there. If you're anything like me, you could be happy cuddling up with Jesus the rest of your life. You'd love to stay. But Jesus tells you, "No, not yet." If you listen, you'll hear his voice telling you to *go*. You've gone through pain. But even in the middle of it, God had a plan. He was preparing you for his purpose. He has a calling on your life. It's time for outrageous obedience to his call. It's time to go.

PART 2

GOD'S FAITHFULNESS FUELS THE MISSION

4

"I Can't Explain It. All the Tests Came Back Clear."

Confidence in God's Faithfulness

She worked as the manager of one of the strip clubs we visit. We'll call her Amber. Hannah, one of my coworkers, and I got to know her quite well. Amber was in her late forties when she had her first child. She had been on drugs during her pregnancy. The baby was born with complications. The doctors told Amber her little boy was blind.

Amber knew we were Christians, so she called us over to her house and asked us to pray over her baby. Hannah and I fasted the day before, asking God to go with us. We weren't praying so much that God would heal the child's eyes, but that he would heal Amber—that he would use this difficult situation to give her spiritual sight.

We went over to Amber's place the next day. It was filthy. I remember stepping over trash strewn on the floor to get to her couch. Frankly, the baby shouldn't have been living in that environment. It felt like the most unlikely place for a child to be healed. But nevertheless, Hannah and I placed our hands over the little baby boy's eyes, and we prayed for God to intervene in his life.

Our visit to Amber's home to pray for her sick child reminded me of another visit to pray for a sick child. . . .

Praying in the Attic

The room smelled like moth balls, and the decor was straight out of 1973. Dark oak paneling stretched down along the angled ceiling toward stacks of books that sat against the short, windowless walls. A lime green shag carpet stretched across the floor. In the corner, across from my dad's desk, sat a matching couch.

I loved going up to that attic office to see my dad. It was in the parsonage next to the little white church, and I'd play up there while my dad studied and prepared his sermons. Lately, though, I hadn't wanted to climb the long staircase up to that attic room. The scleroderma was worse. My hands were curled in, and my toes had curled up, making it painful to walk, much less climb a set of stairs.

James 5:14 says, "Is anyone among you sick? Let them call the elders of the church to pray over them and anoint them with oil in the name of the Lord."

My dad's not a charismatic, but he believes the Bible, and I think he and my mom had come to the end of their rope with my illness. They decided to take that instruction found in James's letter and believe it with an outrageously obedient faith.

So one evening—I remember I was wearing a pink and purple sweater with leggings—I made a painful climb up the stairs to that attic office. I knelt, and Dad touched some olive oil to my forehead. Then he and four of the church's elders knelt around me, placed their hands on my back, and prayed for my healing.

I don't recall anything they said or that anything felt particularly spiritual. I just remember thinking, *It hurts so bad. When is this going to be over?* And yet those men prayed and believed. They kept on praying and believing. They believed God would heal me. And you know, though I was only nine years old and didn't fully understand what was going on, I believed too.

Faithful to Keep His Promises

What do you believe about God healing people?

"When it comes to physical healing," writes pastor Andrew Wilson, "the extremes are relatively easy to see."[1] He's right, you know. Wilson continues:

> We have the loony prosperity gospel preachers and their shallow messages of permanent health and wealth for everyone who follows Jesus. Then we have the starchy cynics who think that everyone who claims to have experienced divine healing is either lying or delusional.[2]

A biblical approach to healing lies somewhere in between.

1. Andrew and Rachel Wilson, *The Life We Never Expected: Hopeful Reflections on the Challenges of Parenting Children with Special Needs* (Wheaton, IL: Crossway, 2016), 109.
2. Wilson and Wilson, *The Life We Never Expected*, 109.

I wonder if what you believe about God healing people says something about what you believe about God's faithfulness? I'm not sure. But I do know we can trust God to do what he says he will do.

James's instruction about calling the elders to pray for those who are sick comes with a promise that we should believe. James writes, "The prayer offered in faith will make the sick person well; the Lord will raise them up" (5:15). James doesn't say the prayer offered in faith *might* make the sick person well; he says the prayer offered in faith *will* make that person well.

Sometimes I'll feel a cold coming on and send up a quick prayer. Then God responds by strengthening my immune system to fight the infection. Other times, Jesus works through doctors, medicine, vaccines, and therapies—restoring our bodies through the care of trained healers. Then there are those moments, usually when a disease is more serious, when pastors and elders are called to bedsides, quiet rooms, or upstairs attics to pray over the sick.

Even when God doesn't answer according to our expectations or timetable, his promise for those who are sick still holds.

God might respond to fervent prayers immediately, erasing the bleeding from the brain scan and putting the cancer in remission. Other times, the illness takes a sudden turn for the worse, and it seems even the prayers of the righteous have gone unanswered. I've prayed for women who our ministry has served who later died because of their addictions. But even when God doesn't answer according to our expectations or timetable, his promise for those who are sick still holds. For those who cling to Christ in faith, there is coming a day—even if it's only in the resurrection—when "the Lord *will* raise them up."

Faithful in Our Desperation

When we left that attic room, my dad and the other elders couldn't know what my immediate fate would be. Scleroderma is a grim diagnosis. I still have scarring on my body, and though people can live with the disease for a long time—because there is medicine today—that wasn't necessarily the case when I was diagnosed. The doctors feared the hardening might spread to my lungs and impact my breathing, or to other organs and cause worse damage or even death.

My family and the elders continued to cry out to God in desperation. We kept seeking medical help as well. Every six months we traveled to the children's hospital for blood work and other tests.

In some ways, my memories of the children's hospital are positive. I got all the popsicles and pudding I could want, and there were toy installations on the walls and play areas designed just for nine-year-olds like me. The hospital staff made the environment as fun and welcoming as they could. But just as vividly as the popsicles, I remember the blood work and choking down the metallic barium so the doctors could scan and measure whether my esophagus was hardening. The repeated tests just reinforced the abnormality of my life and my desperate need for healing.

My physician at the children's hospital was an older woman with a long career. During my next hospital stay, after I'd been in the hospital for more than a week, she came into my room. She looked at my parents and said, "I don't know if we got the tests wrong. I don't know what's going on, but all her levels are perfect. It's like she doesn't even have this disease." Then she hesitated and suggested, "I think we need to do the tests again."

Dad just smiled and said confidently, "She's healed." He knew his prayers had been answered. Then he added, almost laughing, "But, yeah, go ahead and do the tests again." On the day when the results of the second set of tests were ready, our family was ushered into an examination room where we waited to hear from the doctor. Mom sat on the table beside me—she was always close to me—and Dad stood against the wall. When the doctor came in, she said, "I can't explain it. I've never seen this in the history of my practice. But all the tests came back clear."

> "I can't explain it. I've never seen this in the history of my practice. But all the tests came back clear."

My doctor may not have been able to explain it, but we could. In James 5:16, God promises, "Confess your sins to each other and pray for each other so that you may be healed. The prayer of a righteous person is powerful and effective."

God did not need to heal me to prove he's faithful. He *is* faithful. He has continually and sufficiently proven that throughout history. But his healing me was a reminder—yet another confirmation. And we were, once again, thankful for his faithfulness.

When I think back on the miracle God worked for me, I wonder, *Why do we wait until end-of-the-rope desperation to come to God?* I wonder if God allows severe suffering in our lives as a catalyst to move us to that point of desperation. He puts us in a place where we'll rely more fully on Christ.

Faithful, Even for the Faithless

Hannah and I prayed for Amber's baby, encouraged Amber, and then made our way back through the trash and out to our car.

The next day, Amber and her son went to the children's hospital for some extensive eye exams. Midmorning my phone buzzed. "You're never going to believe this!" shouted Amber. "The doctor says the baby can see; there's nothing wrong with his eyes!" Then Amber added, "God did that."

That's the first time Amber had ever spoken about God's work in our presence. She didn't say, "Rachelle, you and Hannah did that." No, she knew. *God did it.* You see, God doesn't merely show his faithfulness to those who are already faithful, to those who are persistent in their trust and obedience. No, our faithful God showed his faithfulness to—and kept his promises for—an undeserving woman who was living far from him.

The book of Hosea begins with the Lord speaking to the prophet and commanding him, "Go, marry a promiscuous woman and have children with her" (Hosea 1:2). The Hebrew word translated "promiscuous" is used throughout the Old Testament to refer to prostitution.[3] On his own,

3. Douglas K. Stuart, "Introduction to Hosea," *NIV Zondervan Study Bible*, ed. D. A. Carson (Grand Rapids: Zondervan, 2015), 1717.

would Hosea have chosen the prostitute Gomer? Probably not. But God told him, "This is who I want you to marry. She is the one I want you to pursue."

Hosea kept on pursuing her, even though after the marriage, Gomer left him to take up with another man. "Love her," God told him, "as the LORD loves the Israelites, though they turn to other gods" (Hosea 3:1). Hosea brought Gomer silver and barley to win her back. He took her in and took care of her. It's a prophetic picture and illustration of how God chose us and continues to pursue us even when we run away from him.

I'm obsessed with an old book by Francine Rivers. It's a fictionalized account of the Hosea story set in an 1850s California casino. The book is entitled *Redeeming Love*, and it isn't small; it's something like five hundred pages long. I started reading it for the first time just before my husband and I left for a tenth-anniversary cruise to the Bahamas. I literally wouldn't get off the ship because I wanted to read that book. Josh kept saying, "Let's go on this excursion!" And I was like, "Nope. I just need a deck chair. Right now, I'm reading this book." (Poor Josh.)

What I love most about *Redeeming Love* is that once Angel, the Gomer figure in the story, is reconciled to her husband, she goes back to rescue another young woman from prostitution. Rivers tells it this way:

> Angel bit her lip. It was like looking in a mirror and seeing herself ten years ago, but she couldn't just stand here, drowning in pain. She had to get this child out of here. Now. She came forward quickly. "It's all right, sweetheart. I'm Angel, and you're coming with me." She

held out her hand. "Come on now. . . . We haven't much time."[4]

Angel's determination flowed out of a confidence that a loving rescue was possible. After all, she'd experienced it. You see, our own faithfulness in the mission begins with knowing and experiencing the depth of God's faithfulness to us.

I often say that my husband is my Hosea. Josh never dated another girl before me. He was this great guy on the football team, but he'd never even held a girl's hand. And, well, I didn't quite have the same experience; I dated lots of guys. I was an angry teenager, doing whatever I wanted and rebelling against the way my parents raised me. Josh knew me for two years before we started dating, and he watched me go through several bad relationships with boys who were on drugs, partying, and certainly were not Christians.

> **That's what God does for us. We might doubt him or be angry with him, but he still patiently pursues us.**

Yet Josh pursued me, and God pursued me through him. When I was faithless, Josh remained faithful. He continually chose to love me and would not let me go.

It's the same with our God. That's what God does for us. We might doubt him or be angry with him, but he still patiently pursues us.

God is faithful and true from the beginning to the end. He's faithful to show his mercy and grace to believers and

4. Francine Rivers, *Redeeming Love: A Novel* (Sisters, OR: Multnomah, 1997), 414.

nonbelievers alike. As 2 Peter 3:9 says, "The Lord is not slow in keeping his promise, as some understand slowness. Instead he is patient with you, not wanting anyone to perish, but everyone to come to repentance." Like Hosea pursued Gomer, God is patiently pursuing and loving you with his redeeming love.

You don't have to be miraculously healed as a child to place your confidence in God. Whatever your story, you can take God's faithfulness to the bank and trust in his relentless pursuit of you. If it hasn't already, everything he has said will come true.

In the introduction of this book, I told the story of a group of women who approached me at a conference. One asked, "Do you think it's too late for me to be used by God?" I told her no, and this is the reason: No matter who we are, what we've done, where we've been, or how long we've waited, God is and will always remain faithful. We may not feel worthy to minister on his behalf, but our ministering is based on his worthiness, not ours.

And God's faithfulness fuels our ministry. We need to be outrageously obedient, and we can be because he is outrageously faithful. At Scarlet Hope, our ministry to women in the adult entertainment industry, we urgently pursue women who are lost. God pursued us when we felt unworthy, and so we pursue women who feel unworthy. Even when they tell us they hate us or don't want anything to do with us, we continue to pursue them. We go into the clubs to love hurting women because we know that's how God first loved us (1 John 4:19). We're motivated to go into hard places and chase down those living in the dark because we know that's how God pursued us.

How about you?

Because God is faithful, you can go too. If you're still breathing, God is not done with you. Every day God gives you is a day he's prepared to show you that he is good and that he has prepared you to go.

5

"Honey, I'm Going to a Strip Club."

Assurance in God's Call

You are called to go.

Jesus commissioned you: "All authority in heaven and on earth has been given to me. Therefore go and make disciples of all nations, baptizing them in the name of the Father and of the Son and of the Holy Spirit, and teaching them to obey everything I have commanded you. And surely I am with you always, to the very end of the age" (Matthew 28:18–20).

You are called to obey. Will you obey Jesus, no matter what?

You are called to go. But *where* are you called to go? And to whom?

Figuring that out can be intimidating, but it doesn't need to be, because God is overseeing the whole process and will use it to deliver you to the people and the place he has for you. In Philippians 1:19, Paul writes, "I know that through your prayers and God's provision of the Spirit of Jesus Christ what has happened to me will turn out for my deliverance." Paul was looking for deliverance—to be rescued—from prison. Some of us need to be rescued from purposelessness.

Want to hear something cool? Paul was confident because of their "prayers and God's *provision* of the Spirit." The root word from which we get "provision" is the same word from which we get "cho-reography." I love that so much. It's like there's a supernatural dance between God and the Holy Spirit in your life. They are moving in and with you. And your prayers work in choreography with the Holy Spirit. It may feel like what's happened is random and what's going to happen is unknown, but no, God is the great choreographer. God has planned out your steps (Proverbs 16:9), and if you'll follow, he'll lead you in a dance that will lead you to your purpose.

> The root word from which we get "provision" is the same word from which we get "choreography." I love that so much. It's like there's a supernatural dance between God and the Holy Spirit in your life.

Turn From or Toward?

In my early twenties, I was confident God was calling me to a difficult place. I knew God had healed me as a child; he had sustained my life for a purpose. I just couldn't figure out what I was supposed to do or where I was supposed to do it.

I found myself working a series of unrelated jobs. You should have seen my résumé!

- dental assistant
- account manager
- makeup artist (at a local media company)
- founder/owner of a catering company

Do you know what the jobs of dental assistant, account manager, makeup artist, and catering company owner have in common? Neither do I. I worked with root canal patients nervously sitting in seats, spreadsheets, blotting sheets, and sheet cakes. I was all over the place.

Maybe you can relate? What I really wanted was to know God's plan, but when it came to discerning his specific purpose for ministry, I was lost.

I was lost, *but* I was open. I was seeking.

I mentioned that around this time my husband and I moved to a suburb of Louisville, Kentucky, in Southern Indiana, where Josh had taken a job at a local church.

I was twenty-one years old and started serving with the church's youth and college ministries. I was unsure where else God wanted me to serve, but even more I was confused by the church. I loved the people, but again and again I found myself asking, "Why does everyone involved in these ministries already know the Lord? Where are the people who are far from God? Are we really engaging in the mission Jesus gave us to seek and save the lost?"

One memory encapsulates the frustration I felt. At our church, there was a mom who liked to chat each Sunday as she dropped off her kids in the youth ministry. One day she asked me, "You know that place over on Veteran's Parkway up on the hill?"

She was talking about a truck stop adult bookstore and sex shop.

"You know, it has that big fluorescent sign out there," she pressed.

"Yep, I know it."

"Oh, that place is disgusting! Every time we drive past it, I tell my kids to turn their heads and look away; those people and what they do are disgusting."

I think back on that woman turning her head away from sin, and my mind floods with images from the Bible. Like when Jesus approached Jerusalem, the city that had rejected God and would see him crucified, and when he "saw the city, he wept over it" (Luke 19:41). Jesus didn't turn away; he looked at Jerusalem, in all its sin, and his heart broke. I also think of the rich young ruler who rejected Jesus because he loved money. Did Jesus turn away? No. "Jesus looked at him and loved him" (Mark 10:21). Or what about the father in Jesus's story of the prodigal son who wasted his life in sinful living? Did the father, who represents God, consider his son disgusting? Did he turn away? No, day after day he stared longingly into the distance, hoping to see his sinful son coming down the street. And when that day finally arrived? "But while he was still a long way off, his father saw him and was filled with compassion for him; he ran to his son, threw his arms around him and kissed him" (Luke 15:20).

I wonder, when it comes to sinners and sinful places, do you turn your head away like that mom in my church? Or do you run to them in compassion and tears and love?

Searching for a People

Around that same time, I hosted a Bible study group of college girls at our apartment. Together in our living room, we studied the book of Esther. It's a theological and literary masterpiece that recounts how a young Jewish orphan rose from obscurity to become King Xerxes's queen and then the rescuer of her people. God's name never appears in the book, but even the smallest details of Esther's story testify to God's providence.

One emphasis in our Bible study was Esther's relationship with her people. When the young girl was first taken into the king's harem, she didn't reveal her nationality and family background (Esther 2:10). Her ethnic identity remained unknown when the evil Haman planned to wipe out the Jews with a murderous genocide. When Esther found out about the plot, she had a choice: Would she choose the safer and more comfortable path? Or would she identify with her people and risk her life for them?

Esther's relative, Mordecai, sent word for her "to go into the king's presence to beg for mercy and plead with him for *her people*" (Esther 4:8, emphasis added). He told her, "Who knows but that you have come to your royal position for such a time as this?" (Esther 4:14).

I had already been asking, "Where are the people who need Jesus in our church? Where are the people who don't know him? Why are we turning our heads away from them instead of toward them? Why are we waiting for them to come to us?" But after working through that study, I began praying, "God, how can you use me like you used Esther?

Will you give me a people? God, please show me the people to whom you are sending me."

Honestly, I wondered, *Should I go to India? Maybe Africa?* As a web designer, Josh knew he could work pretty much anywhere. He told me, "Wherever God calls you, I'll go." We wrestled with those questions every day. I'm sure I was driving my husband up the wall. But I didn't know where that *wherever* was. I needed to find my purpose and my people.

If you're not sure where and to whom God has called you, are you asking those questions?

Joining God Where He Is at Work

If you *are* asking those questions, how do you get an answer? You listen.

God has pursued you, and so your passion should be to pursue him, and he will show you how to pursue others. God has proven himself faithful, and his faithfulness fuels you. With the assurance that God has a plan and is calling, you *listen*.

Henry Blackaby once wrote, "We don't choose what we will do for God; He invites us to join Him where He wants to involve us."[1] I love that. Pastor Blackaby's statement about God's invitation is built on a series of important convictions:[2]

- First, "God is always at work around you." He is already up to something!

1. Henry Blackaby, Richard Blackaby, and Claude King, *Experiencing God: Knowing and Doing the Will of God*, rev. ed. (Nashville: B&H, 2008), 72.
2. Blackaby, Blackaby, and King, *Experiencing God*, 51–64.

- Second, because God loves us in a "real and personal way," we can count on the fact that he wants us "to become involved with Him in His work." We don't have to manufacture a ministry or concoct a calling. God is inviting us into his work. He will speak to us—through his Word, through his people, through his Spirit, and through our circumstances—to call us to join him where he's already working in the world.

- Third, following that invitation will mean making a choice. Just as it did with Esther, God's invitation for us to work with him "always leads you to a crisis of belief that requires faith and action." It will require courage, and you may need to "make major adjustments in your life to join God in what He is doing."[3]

Looking back at that time in my life, I think I had a couple things going for me.

First, I was asking God to point me to his purpose for me, and I was listening. I'm not sure if God will speak if we're not asking, and I don't think we will hear him if we are not listening.

Second, I was going while I was waiting. Too often, when we don't know exactly what God has for us, we do nothing. We say we're waiting for direction but, well, you can't steer a parked car. Right? If you are still in park, you're not going anywhere. But if you start moving, even if you are going the wrong way, you can make changes along the road and get yourself going in the right direction. It's like when

---

3. Blackaby, Blackaby, and King, *Experiencing God*, 64.

your Google Maps says, "Rerouting." In my early twenties, I was frustrated because I wasn't sure what God had for me to do. But while I waited, I served in our church's youth and college ministries, fed and cared for homeless people, and led mission trips—all good things. In fact, it was in leading that college Bible study that God spoke to me about where and to whom I should go.

> Too often, when we don't know exactly what God has for us, we do nothing. We would say we're waiting for direction but, well, you can't steer a parked car.

Jesus made an amazing promise: "And surely I am with you always, to the very end of the age" (Matthew 28:20). It's incredible that he offers that kind of intimacy and guidance. It's amazing that he promises to always be with us. But have you ever thought about the context of that promise? It starts out, "Therefore go . . ." (Matthew 28:19). Jesus assures us of his presence *within the context of our going.*

I wonder if it's only as we are going that we discover where we're to go. I'm not sure, but I do know that when we receive the call, we are confronted with a choice.

God brought me to that crisis of belief one morning as I was driving to work. Each day, I'd get into my red 2002 Ford Focus hatchback, hop on the interstate, and drive the four exits from our apartment in Southern Indiana into the city. Just before I crossed over the Ohio River into Louisville, I'd pass a strip club called Mystic.

One morning, God turned my heart toward it. It felt like I had been asking and listening forever, then God responded in an instant. He impressed on my heart, "I'm sending you there—to those people—to share my hope and my love."

It was like God himself was sitting beside me!

I immediately reached over into the console, picked up my Nokia flip phone (you know, because iPhones didn't exist yet), and dialed Josh.

I told him, "God's calling me to take the gospel to the women in the strip clubs. Honey, I'm *going* to a strip club!" He could hear in my voice that as surely as the sky is blue, this is what God had told me to do. I didn't know how he'd respond, but he simply said, "That's exactly what Jesus would do."

Josh always had this sense that God had saved me from my childhood illness for a specific purpose. He reminded me of what I'd been studying with those college girls—how God had called Esther "for such a time as this." Finally, *this* time had come. Honestly, we didn't know exactly what that call meant, but we knew God was calling.

Learning about the Need

I heard God's voice, but I was naïve. I didn't know the difference between an adult bookstore and a strip club. I thought all the dancers in the clubs were also prostitutes. I had no idea about traffickers. I knew nothing, but I could not wait to learn. I immediately went online at the office that day and began to do research. I probably should have been concerned about what my bosses would think of my search history, but I couldn't turn my gaze away. A new world of lostness opened to me, and all I wanted to do was look at it with compassion, tears, and love.

Through web searches, I learned that my little Kentucky city—not Vegas or Atlantic City or Miami—had *twenty-seven* strip clubs and *over forty* illegal massage parlors. You might think your town doesn't have such dark places, but it does. Everything that happens in Vegas is in your town too. It's just not on Main Street or celebrated publicly the way it is in Sin City.

I was discovering new information, but really it had been right in front of my eyes the whole time. I had driven by that strip club/sex shop on my way to and from work every day. I had ignored it, but now I couldn't stop thinking about the women working there. Who were they? Was their life like the movie *Pretty Woman*? How did they get to where they were? Did they know about the God who created and loved them?

And I couldn't get the voice of the woman from my church—*Oh, that place is disgusting*—out of my head. Her words and the Spirit's call were all the push I needed to keep researching and then to start coming up with a plan.

A couple of friends and I started doing prayer drives around the local strip clubs. We would drive to a club and pray for God to open a door for us so that we could visit the women inside and share the hope of Christ with them. We prayed every Tuesday night, waiting for God to tell us what to do next.

About a year later, I found myself driving a couple of hours to attend a workshop on human trafficking at a church in Lexington. Today, human trafficking is a well-known justice issue. There are entire advocacy groups and even public service announcements on television and

YouTube that warn about it.[4] But back in 2008 when some friends and I attended that workshop, it wasn't talked about at all. I thought about the sex trade as something that happened "over there" in another country, but a 2005 study estimated that even back then there were already between four and eight thousand women working in the sex industry in conservative little Bible-Belt Kentucky.[5]

In the middle of that workshop, I heard the Spirit prompt me again, "Stop praying. It's time to go." The woman at my church had told her kids to look away, but you better believe I looked. Others told me not to go, but Jesus said I should, and there was no stopping me.

After calling multiple churches in the area to see if any were reaching the adult entertainment industry in our city (they weren't), and after a year of research and praying outside of several strip clubs (I'll tell you that story in chapter 9), Sarah and I followed Jesus into the dark. The workshop was on a Sunday. On the following Tuesday (as I described in chapter 2), we entered our first club, under the black lights, to share the hope and love of Jesus with the women working there.

4. A more recent 2018 Kentucky state report on human trafficking identified forty-one human trafficking businesses, 106 traffickers, and 377 victims in our state. See *Kentucky Spotlight: 2018 National Human Trafficking Hotline Statistics*, https://humantraffickinghotline.org/sites/default/files/KY-2018-State-Report.pdf.

As of 2019, Kentucky ranked 25th in the US for the number of active criminal human trafficking cases making their way through the federal courts. See "Kentucky State Summary," *The Human Trafficking Institute* (2019), https://traffickinginstitute.org/wp-content/uploads/2022/01/Kentucky-2019-State-Summary.pdf and "Criminal Record Relief for Trafficking Survivors," *Polaris Project* (October 2019), https://polarisproject.org/wp-content/uploads/2019/10/2019-CriminalRecordRelief-Kentucky.pdf.

5. Gary Potter, "Prostitution and the Sex Industry in Kentucky," *Kentucky Justice & Safety Research Bulletin*, vol. 7, no. 1, 2005, encompass.eku.edu/kjsrb/4.

God's People Help Us to Discern His Voice

I've come to think of clarifying God's calling a bit like putting together a puzzle. God knows the big picture, but we can only put it together piece by piece. We don't do that on our own. God guides the whole process by speaking to us through:

- his Word (as he did when he used that Esther Bible study to prompt me to pray)
- his Spirit (as he did on my morning commute to work)
- circumstances (as he did in my childhood illness and in the example and stories of my father)

God also speaks to us through *his people*. God loves us and will sometimes use people in our lives to help guide us into his plan and purpose.

He did that with me toward the beginning of our ministry. I had attended the trafficking workshop with a group of women who were my compatriots and partners in research and prayer for the people in the clubs and adult entertainment industry. On the way back from the workshop, I told them—Sarah, Jennifer, and Chloe—that I'd felt the Spirit say, "It's time to go." Then I asked them to fast and pray with me about which of the twenty-seven clubs we should go into. Honestly, I had it in my head that we should take our first meal to the women in a particular club near downtown Louisville. But after fasting and praying, God had put it on my friends' hearts that we should go to a different club, Fantasy X.

We'd held most of our prayer meetings at a Wendy's right across the street from the Fantasy X club, so it made more sense to them that we should start there. When the day came to go to the first club, the one I'd chosen was closed. I was frustrated at the time. But looking back, I feel like the enemy was using the other club as a distraction. It was at Fantasy X (the club I described in chapter 2) that the door for our ministry first opened. Our ministry didn't begin serving meals in the club near downtown for seven more years. If circumstances and those other women hadn't been there helping me to hear God's call with clarity, our ministry may never have gotten off the ground.

> If you are still trying to discern your calling, do you have some people who are listening to God and speaking to you on his behalf?

If you are still trying to discern your calling, do you have some people who are listening to God and speaking to you on his behalf? It can make all the difference.

How about You?

God has called you. He's called you to the lost, to the least, to the last in, and to the left out. He tells us in Isaiah 1:17, "Learn to do right; seek justice. Defend the oppressed. Take up the cause of the fatherless; plead the case of the widow." Being justice-minded is not just a suggestion but a command from the Lord.

In chapter 4, I wrote about how mission begins with having confidence in God's faithfulness. We must know that God keeps his promises, that he's faithful even in our faithlessness. That belief in God's faithfulness should fuel us. God is faithful to us, and we need to be faithful to God's call on our lives. Faith that is passive is faithless. We'll explore this more in chapter 7; with all the heroes of the faith in Hebrews 11, we see that faith always *acts*.

Some Christian women read devotional books and attend Bible studies, and that is literally the sum total of their discipleship. That's all they do. Later in the book, I'll explore some of the barriers that keep us from embracing outrageous obedience when we hear God's call. But for now, I want to encourage you. If you've heard God's Spirit prompting you, don't ignore it. Don't close your ears to his voice. If there's a people or a place on your heart, don't look away. Don't wait for someone else to do it. Don't worry about all the details of how. Instead, find your assurance in the Lord.

People have asked me, "What drove you to go into a strip club?" I really can't say anything other than the Holy Spirit and how I was raised. There's nothing good in me that makes me particularly fit for this work. But God, in his faithfulness, prepared me with a conviction that he's always at work around me. Then he prompted me to go. He saved me from my disease and then put a burden on my heart for a particular people.

What is the Spirit saying to you? Who are the people he is putting on your heart? Let me demystify the idea of calling for you. You probably won't hear God's audible voice, but if I had to guess, I bet you already know who *your people* are. You can already tell me who it is for whom you have the greatest burden.

Sometimes . . .

- There are people in our lives for whom God has given us greater responsibility—like an aging parent or our young children.
- God just puts people in our path—like when my dad met Steven at the gas station.
- God sends people to a particular place—like Paul's longing for Spain (see Romans 15) or missionary Katie Davis Majors, whom God sent to Uganda as a teenager.

Whoever your people are, commit your burden to God and let him guide you to risk-taking faith. If your desire for mission aligns with his Word and is affirmed by godly people in your life, then you can believe that the call is from him. He may call you to go to someone from whom others are turning their heads. But even though the path may be difficult—even though it will require risk—he will go before you, behind you, and around you. Be assured that if Christ has called you, he will fill you with his Spirit for the work.

6

"I Don't Think I Can Do That Sober."

*How the Savior's Love Leads Us
to Risk-Taking Faith*

I t was a typical Thursday night at the club for our ministry team. We arrived at 8:30 p.m., unloaded our food, and set up in front of the DJ booth. We'd prepared a crowd favorite that night: fried chicken and mashed potatoes, rolls, salad, and mac and cheese—enough to feed thirty dancers and ten bouncers.

About twenty minutes later, I noticed a woman walk in the door. After serving at the club week after week, we began to know each employee and regular pretty well. This woman was clearly new, and she looked utterly lost. She wore jeans and a blue sweater draped off her shoulder. She carried a large bag with clothes spilling out of it. I didn't know if she worked there or was a patron, but God calls us to serve every person he puts in our path.

As soon as I saw her, I walked over to her. As I approached, the woman staggered and bumped into a barstool. She was drunk. So drunk she could barely stay on her feet and hold on to her bag.

The alcohol not only impacted this woman's balance, it also gave her the courage to talk. I invited this woman to get something to eat, and she asked me how much the meal cost. As soon as I told her the meal was free, she made her way over to our table, and with hesitation in her eyes, she began to tell me her story.

"You know," she said, "I've never worked here before, but I have five children who haven't eaten in a week, and I'm desperate. My friend told me I could make fast money at the club, so I walked here to apply."

"What does it take to try out?" I asked.

With desperate eyes, she told me the manager had explained that she would have to dance in front of him and the rest of the staff completely nude.

She then told the manager, "I don't think I can do that sober." The manager suggested she go to the bar for a few drinks, to find some "liquid courage." That's exactly what she'd done.

Bravery Born from Desperation

Courage is the mental or moral strength to venture forward, persevere, and withstand danger or difficulty. In a sense, the woman I met that night at the club was courageous. You've got to be brave to dance naked in front of a room full of people, but her courage was born out of desperation. She was a young mother who was desperate enough to sacrifice her dignity to feed her children.

When I think about that mother's courage, I'm reminded of another needy woman. We meet her in Luke 8:42–48, where we learn she's been subject to bleeding for twelve years. In Bible times, she would have been seen as unclean, untouchable, and perhaps even unlovable. She was anxious for healing and must have tried every means of help to which she had access. I can imagine her face, full of shame and embarrassment. I think she and the drunk mother in the club that night probably had a lot in common.

Sadly, I don't think this sick woman's struggle was a secret. When we meet her, there's a huge crowd between her and Jesus, and we get the idea that everyone knew about her illness. Even so, despite her shame, this woman acted with bravery and faith. She believed Jesus could heal her, and her courage compelled her to fight through the pressing crowd to touch the edge of Jesus's cloak—just for the chance she might find healing.

> Everyone in the crowd would have considered her unclean and unfit to be there. But the bleeding woman summoned up all the courage she could because she knew she needed Christ.

I love the risk she was willing to take. Everyone in the crowd would have considered her unclean and unfit to be there. But the bleeding woman summoned up all the courage she could because she knew she needed Christ.

Sometimes I wonder how many modern-day Christians would be willing to take that sort of risk. Would we even think it was worth it? Would we believe healing could come just by touching the hem of his garment? Have we ever been that desperate?

If the bleeding woman was seen as unclean and unlovable, exploited women feel the desperation tenfold. Studies find that survivors of trafficking for sexual exploitation are likely to have experienced several types of trauma that make them particularly vulnerable:

- In Connecticut, 86 of the 88 identified victims had a history with child welfare services as well.[1]

- In Ohio, 40 percent had a history of sexual abuse by family members, and 63 percent had run away from home at least once.[2]

- In Hawaii, 63 percent came from the foster care system.[3]

- In San Diego, California, 55 percent came from homelessness.[4]

1. Connecticut Department of Children and Families, *A Child Welfare Response to Domestic Minor Sex Trafficking*, 2012, https://portal.ct.gov/-/media/dcf /HumanTrafficking/pdf/ResponsetoDomesticMinotSexTraffickingpdf.

2. C. Williamson, T. Perdue, L. Belton, and O. Burns, *Domestic Sex Trafficking in Ohio: Final Report*, (Ohio Human Trafficking Commission, 2012), https:// www.ohioattorneygeneral.gov/getattachment/27542187-0e4d-4d48-9b47 -8ecbe6ed21b2/2012-Domestic-Sex-Trafficking-in-Ohio-Report.aspx.

3. D. Roe-Sepowitz and K. Jabola-Carolus, *Sex Trafficking in Hawaii: Part II, The Stories of Survivors*, Arizona State University, (Arizona State University Office of Sex Trafficking Intervention and the Hawaii State Commission on the Status of Women, January 2019), https://socialwork.asu.edu/sites/default /files/stir/final_finalexecutive_summary_part_ii_sex_trafficking_in_hawaii _.pdf.

4. Carpenter and Gates, "Nature and Extent."

In a broader 2014 investigation:

- 88 percent of sex trafficking survivors experienced depression.
- 76 percent experienced anxiety.
- 73 percent had nightmares.
- 68 percent had flashbacks.

And though the women were unwilling victims:

- 82 percent of them had feelings of shame or guilt.
- 54 percent experienced post-traumatic stress disorder, and 41 percent had attempted suicide.[5]

Is there any hope we can offer to the victims of such tragedy? Is there a garment hem that's worth the risk of fighting through a crowd to touch?

Hope That's Worth the Risk

In Luke's Gospel, Jesus was on his way to heal Jairus's daughter when the bleeding woman touched him. It would have been easy for him to see her as an interruption. After all, he had an appointment to heal the dying daughter of an important synagogue official. But his agenda and all the other people around him didn't matter in comparison to

5. L. Lederer and C. Wetzel, "The Health Consequences of Sex Trafficking and Their Implications for Identifying Victims in Healthcare Facilities," *Annals of Health Law* 23 (2014), 61–91, https://www.icmec.org/wp-content/uploads/2015/10/Health-Consequences-of-Sex-Trafficking-and-Implications-for-Identifying-Victims-Lederer.pdf.

this one woman. Her risk-taking faith shined brighter than everything else at that moment, and Jesus stopped to recognize it.

He said, "Someone touched me; I know that power has gone out from me" (Luke 8:46). Can you imagine how this woman must have felt at that moment? She had taken such a costly risk and now felt exposed.

How would the Savior respond to her? Jesus then said, "Daughter, your faith has healed you. Go in peace" (Luke 8:48).

I'm amazed by this moment. Don't you just love how Jesus calls her *daughter*? What a gentle and dignifying way for him to speak to a woman who had spent more than a decade as an untouchable outcast. Turns out, his love was worth every courageous step she took.

> Don't you just love how Jesus calls her *daughter*? What a gentle and dignifying way for him to speak to a woman who had spent more than a decade as an untouchable outcast.

When we go into the clubs, we discipline ourselves to have the same attitude toward the dancers that Jesus did toward this woman. We encounter ladies who are deeply broken, but we want to look at them with eyes of love. We want to see them as daughters of the King. No matter what brokenness she may have experienced, when a woman finds faith in Jesus Christ, he heals her, and the Father calls her his daughter. We want every woman we encounter in the clubs to encounter the love of Christ and to see that it's always worth the risk.

The Color of Hope

On the Sunday morning before I met that drunk mother in the club, I ran into a friend at church. He was also the accountant helping us fill out and file the 501c3 application that would make our new ministry an official nonprofit.

"So, have you decided on a name for the ministry yet?" he asked me.

"I never intended to start a nonprofit," I explained, "so I'm still waiting on God to tell me what he wants me to name it." I was quite serious. I had no idea what we'd name the ministry, and I was hoping to hear from the Lord.

"Well, let me know when you have a name," he said and chuckled, "and then I'll submit the paperwork. We can't complete the application without a name."

That afternoon, while I was still pondering what we'd name this ministry, I set aside some time to read and study the Bible. God got my attention with Matthew 27:27–31:

Then the governor's soldiers took Jesus into the Praetorium and gathered the whole company of soldiers around him. They stripped him and put a scarlet robe on him, and then twisted together a crown of thorns and set it on his head. They put a staff in his right hand. Then they knelt in front of him and mocked him. "Hail, king of the Jews!" they said. They spit on him, and took the staff and struck him on the head again and again. After they had mocked him, they took off the robe and put his own clothes on him. Then they led him away to crucify him.

Tears started rolling down my cheeks as I pictured my King being stripped and scorned as the soldiers put a scarlet robe on him. The word *scarlet* struck me. Not only did Jesus wear a scarlet robe, but that robe would also be stained scarlet with his blood. Jesus was a different kind of king— not the kind who ruled with wealth and oppressive power, but the sort who courageously laid down his life to save us from our brokenness and sin (see Romans 5:8). There's hope in the blood of Jesus, poured out for all people, that's worth taking a risk for. It's worth stepping out with risk-taking faith.

As I read, the name for our new ministry came to me. I stood up and bolted into the next room to tell my husband, "The Lord spoke to me. We're going to call the ministry Scarlet Hope!"

Josh smiled. "I like it," he said. "Let's pray about it for a few days, and if your mind is not changed, we can fill out the paperwork."

Courageous Faith, Born of the Spirit

"Courage," wrote G. K. Chesterton, "is almost a contradiction in terms. It means a strong desire to live taking the form of a readiness to die."[6] When people hear that I go into strip clubs to share the gospel, they often say, "That's really courageous. I could never do that." Then they follow that statement up by asking the oddest question: "Do you feel safe?" My answer is always the same: "Of course not." But that's the point. It's outrageous obedience.

Courageous faith rarely feels safe. It's what Ed McCully, classmate of Jim Elliot, described as living "a life of reckless abandon for the Lord, putting all my energy and strength

6. G. K. Chesterton, *Orthodoxy* (San Francisco: Ignatius Press, 1908, 1995), 99.

into it."[7] Truly, it's a risk. You don't know all the pieces of the puzzle or even what the picture will look like once it's put together. Courageous faith means trusting Christ enough to keep stepping out even when you can't see how things will turn out.

I have heard it said, from a quote widely attributed to Winston Churchill, that fear is a reaction and courage is a decision. I believe courage *is* a decision that is rooted in God's Word and born of God's Spirit. Courageous faith is a course we choose. It requires that we participate in God's will, that we decide to act in accordance with what he's called us to do. As Elisabeth Elliot shared, "You either line yourself up with the Son of God and say to the Father, 'Thy will be done,' or you capitulate to the principle which governs the rest of the world and you say, 'My will be done.'"[8]

> They ask the oddest question: "Do you feel safe?" My answer is always the same: "Of course not."

Courage is a woman deciding after twenty-three years of dancing in a club to put her faith in Christ, walk out of the club, and leave that life behind. Courage is a woman getting her GED and going to college for the first time at age forty-five. Courage is a woman who chooses to give her baby life even though most of the voices around her say to abort. Courage is women walking through the door of a

---

7. Ed McCully, Ed McCully to Jim Elliot, September 22, 1950, quoted in Elisabeth Elliot, *Through Gates of Splendor*, 40th Anniversary Edition (Nashville: Tyndale Momentum, 1981), 51.

8. Elisabeth Elliot, "The Glory of God's Will," presented at the Urbana Missions Conference in Urbana, IL, in December 1976, Urbana Missions video posted June 16, 2015, https://www.youtube.com/watch?v=8HzO3gevgE0.

strip club and telling both dancers and owners that Jesus sent them. It's loving someone who may hate you and even spit in your face. It could even be as simple as telling a friend about Jesus. And courage, when you've been bleeding for years, is walking through a crowd just to clutch the hem of Jesus's cloak.

You can courageously choose to follow God's call even when it doesn't feel safe. Why? Because Jesus has called you his daughter, and he has given you his Spirit. On one hand, being in the center of God's will is never safe; there's always risk involved. On the other hand, when you've spent time in God's Word and heard his clear call, you can rest assured that he will provide by his Spirit all the strength you'll need for the journey. He promises to always be with you.

As Corrie ten Boom wrote, "Trying to do the Lord's work in your own strength is the most confusing, exhausting and tedious of all work. But when you are filled with the Holy Spirit, then the ministry of Jesus just flows out of you."[9]

How about you? Where are you seeking courage? Do you look within yourself for strength and hope, or to the one who bled and died for you? Is your vision limited to what you can see, or do you believe he has a greater purpose? Are you looking for comfort and safety, or are you willing to believe that if God sends you on stony paths, he'll provide strong shoes?[10] Do you trust that if God has called you to go, you can count on his promise to be with you?

9. Corrie ten Boom and Jamie Buckingham, *Tramp for the Lord* (New York: Berkley, 1974), 57.
10. "If God sends us on stony paths, he provides strong shoes" is often attributed to Corrie ten Boom, but it is most likely from the original, "If God sends us

What's in a Name?

The woman I met that Thursday night was in a particularly dark place. With the state she was in, I couldn't help but wonder whether her poverty had come as the consequence of an addiction. But at that moment, what led her to a place of desperation didn't matter; she just needed a glimpse of hope.

"I'm so thankful I met you," I told the woman as I helped her to the serving line. "I don't think it's an accident that we're both here tonight."

The woman smiled, and I began to make her a plate. But as I began to serve her, I saw that she had leaned over the mac and cheese pan and begun scooping it directly into her mouth. My heart sank; she was poor, drunk, *and* hopelessly hungry.

I took the pan of mac and cheese and set it aside for her to take home. As I did, she turned her head away from the food and threw up all down my front. Without even acknowledging what had just happened, she looked up at me with tears in her eyes and asked, "Will you pray for me?" Though this woman had run to the bar to find courage, she knew what she really needed was prayer. Real courage—true faith—comes only by the Spirit.

We were covered with vomit, but God was at work. This woman's plea for me to pray for her was a sign that the Spirit of Christ was doing something in her. As I held the woman's hands and prayed, she dropped to her knees and

---

on stony paths He will provide us with strong shoes," by Alexander MacLaren, "Shod for the Road: An Address on Deuteronomy 33:25" in *Great Sermons by Great Preachers* (Reading, PA: Frank J. Boyer, 1889), 311.

cried out for God to save, rescue, and free her. God used our encounter in the strip club that night to begin a work of salvation in this woman's life and make her a daughter of the King.

After we finished praying, I noticed the lights in the club had come up. The DJ had lowered the music, and everyone was staring at us. The woman didn't seem to notice.

"I met Jesus here tonight," she said. "I have found *hope*!" Her face was filled with peace and her eyes never left mine. She was completely resolute, and my heart was overwhelmed.

In that moment, it felt as if there was no one else but the Lord, this woman, and me in the club. I started telling her more about the gospel, how Christ came to die for her sins, and how believing in him is the only way to heaven.

I talked fast because I knew we didn't have much time. Walking into the club drunk and then retching on the floor wasn't something the management would allow. Sure enough, as I was recounting the gospel story, the manager tapped the woman on her shoulder.

"I'm sorry, this club isn't for you," he said. "I've called you a cab; you're going to have to leave."

My teammates packed up all the remaining food, I quickly wrote down her number, and then we walked with her to the cab, helping carry all of the food we were sending with her for the kids. As we helped her get into the taxi, I asked her name.

She smiled and replied, "My name is Scarlet."

God, you are here.

As her cab drove off, I paused with holy admiration. I needed to change my clothes, but all I could do was stand there amazed by God's all-knowing sovereignty and his love for these women and for me.

Our Savior loves the desperate and exploited. He loves the sin-sick and addicted. He offers the kind of balm that heals trauma and generational sin. He loves us with every ounce of his blood. He risked everything to save us, so how can we not love others with the same sort of risk-taking, courageous faith?

7

"How Do I Trust a God I Can't See?"

*Faith that Faces Down Doubt
and Overcomes Fear*

I was mortified. And embarrassed. But mostly disappointed. I was disappointed in God and, honestly, it created doubt. Those doubts felt smothering, suffocating. The irony is that it all started with such promise.

Scarlet Hope was up and running, and we were praying for a house that would serve as a transitional home for women coming out of the industry. Then I saw it. It seemed perfect because it was so *im*perfect. The abandoned house was only nine hundred square feet. Sure, that was very small, but we had very little money. The house was fairly beaten down, but our faith in our ability to raise enough money to buy a home was strong. After all, the home seemed . . . reasonable.

We started doing prayer circles around the house. When you hear "prayer circles" you probably picture people walking around the house while praying. Yes, that happened. But the house was so small, our team was also able to stand around it in a circle, all holding hands.

I tracked down the owner and met with her several times. Turns out we would need thirty-five thousand dollars to buy the house and forty thousand more to renovate it. It would be seventy-five grand in total. That was a lot, but we felt like it was within the realm of possibility.

So we planned a fundraising gala to raise the money. We've done many since, but this was our first. We were excited and *nervous*. We set a goal of raising the seventy-five thousand dollars, and when the night finally arrived, we raised that exact amount: $75,000.00

The next week I went to the woman who owned the house, announcing we now had the money to buy her property. She said, "No." After having told me she'd sell us the house, she suddenly reversed course and announced that she was going to hold on to it.

I walked away feeling like my faith had been sucker punched. I began to lose faith that God had heard our prayers for this transitional house. I lost faith that God would provide what our ministry needed. Frankly, I was angry at God. And I was embarrassed, because I had stood in front of hundreds of people at the gala and told them God had called us to raise money to buy this house. I felt like I had lied to all those people. I was confused. It had seemed like such a confirmation when we raised the money we needed down to the penny. None of it made sense. The only thing I felt sure of was that God had let me down.

When Doubts Drown Out Your Faith

What do you do when doubts drown out your faith? The temptation for all of us, I think, is to put on a brave face and claim, "I don't struggle with doubt," but we all have times when our faith wavers. Honestly, I don't believe that's a bad thing. Times of testing can grow our faith.

I look back on my journey to when I gave my life to Jesus at the Dairy Queen at eight years of age. At that time, I had a strong but childlike faith. Later, when Josh and I were first married, we stopped going to church. We had to decide whether we would continue to believe what we had been taught and *why* we would believe it. Would we limp along with our parents' faith or really develop our own? Later, when I had miscarriage after miscarriage, I struggled with doubt again.

Each of these trials caused us to dig deeper into God's Word. Wrestling through our doubts led us to own our faith in ways that have built upon what we've inherited.

Over the years, I've also learned that it's not just me. I've found that even if they won't admit it, most everyone has some doubts:

The women I meet in the strip clubs have doubts. Most of the women are very open about it. I think of a dancer I met. She had coarse, frizzy hair, blue eyes, and a bright smile that lit up the room. Her clothes were old and worn. The industry had taken a toll on her body, causing scars and wounds from head to toe. As we talked, I learned her life had been marked with extreme pain. Her father molested her when she was just a young girl, and she was taken away by child protective services and placed in a foster home. Her foster parents beat and abused her when she acted out, so she ran away at age fourteen and encountered streets filled with drugs, thugs, and violence. She was so angry inside that she decided she could fit right in. She continued to be used and abused, but she felt like she had no other options. Fast-forward a decade and she was working in a strip club. One evening, we were able to sit and talk, and I told her about God's love for her. She looked at me in confused disbelief and asked, "How do I trust a God I can't see when the people I can see—people I trusted to love me—treat me poorly and abuse me?"

The women I meet who won't go into the strip clubs have doubts. Most of these women are *not* very open about it. They tell me they're interested in joining our team, but they need every question fully answered before they'll even consider stepping into a club. I tell them that we go in without much of a plan, that we listen to the ladies and to the Holy Spirit. I tell them that we must walk in faith. But for many, that's not sufficient. They fear what might happen. They fear being asked a question or put in a situation that makes them uncomfortable. They fear what other "respectable" people will think of them. Most would not admit this, but it's all a failure to believe. And that's a problem, because it's only when faith overcomes fear that we can follow Jesus in outrageous obedience.

If you let doubts drown out your faith, you will cave in the face of fear. And if fear stops you because doubt has drowned out your faith:

- *You will never feel as close to God as you could.* We know that we should live our lives in dependence on God, but most of us only do what we can do on our own. When this is the case, we don't *really* need God. We're able to live *without* radical reliance. And in so doing we unintentionally keep our God at a distance.
- *You will miss out on having a front-row seat to God's work.* I was recently at a Michael Bublé concert. Josh and I had amazing seats near the stage, and I felt like Michael (I was so close to him that we're now on a first-name basis!) was singing directly to me. The music swept me away to la-la land. My husband tapped me, laughing, and said, "Rachelle, look around, you are the youngest person here by thirty years!" I haven't had a front-row seat at a concert very often, but it's been awesome when I have. You get a better view of everything, and you feel like you are in the action.
- *You will miss out on the most amazing show you will ever see.* When we trust God, he shows up and shows off. Jesus is doing incredible things in the world every single day, but it's those who are following close behind him who get to see it up close.

In 2012, I was in Las Vegas leading some women to do outreach at a strip club. Nine years later, in 2021, I was in Reno and met a woman who had been volunteering at our ministry there. She told me that she had been trafficked earlier in her life and ended up working in a Vegas strip club.

Then one day some women came into her club, and they were gracious. They gave her a free lip gloss. When she got home, she saw that it said "Scarlet Hope" on the tube and had a phone number on it. She did a Google search for "Scarlet Hope," came across a video I had made, and then our website. She eventually decided to move to the closest Scarlet Hope location in Reno, where she met our director there, got involved in a partner church, got married, and is now helping people find freedom from addiction.

> We know that we should live our lives in dependence on God, but most of us only do what we can do on our own. When this is the case, we don't really need God.

It's amazing! The woman thanked me, saying that she credits her story to our walking into the club that night in Vegas. I can't take credit for God's work, but I *love* getting to be a part of the story. I feel close to him when I get a front-row seat to his work.

If you let your doubts drown out your faith, you could miss out on impacting thousands of lives. But you can play an essential part in a God story if you exercise the sort of faith that takes risks and overcomes fear.

Faith Takes Risks

A lot of people think being a Christian means being reasonable and respectable. No. Being a Christian means following Jesus. Jesus didn't get crucified for being reasonable and respectable. Jesus was dangerous. And following him will not make us dignified; it will make us dangerous. Faith is always dangerous because it always leads us to risk.

God doesn't call us to be the same as everyone else. He calls us to be different.

God doesn't call us to keep doing the same thing. He calls us to do something different.

If we're honest, we want the same comforts as everyone else. We want to keep doing the same things we've been doing. But *same* is *safe*, and safe isn't faith-filled. We can't keep living the same way; there's no faith in that. We need to ask God to help us trust him enough to overcome our doubts and jump out in faith. And we can. We can have that kind of faith because God is faithful.

Faith is always dangerous because it always leads us to risk. God doesn't call us to be the same as everyone else. He calls us to be different.

When Christian author Henri Nouwen was in his late sixties, he went to see the Flying Rodleighs, a trapeze troupe. He watched, incredulous, at their high-flying act. He looked around and saw everyone was equally enraptured by the performance. As he watched others in the audience, he noticed they were all focused on the flyer, the person who dives through the air, and no one was paying attention to the catcher. But he realized that the flyer wouldn't dare take the risk without the confidence he would be caught. It's the catcher who allows the amazing to happen.

Nouwen knew someone who worked with the Flying Rodleighs, and after the show, he invited Nouwen to try the trapeze himself. They put a harness on him, and the trapeze artist told Nouwen, "The flyer must never catch the catcher. . . . He must wait in absolute trust."[1] Then, this elderly, former Harvard professor flew through the air giggling. Nouwen was thrown through the air again and again by the trapeze artist. Knowing he was truly safe allowed him to take what would have otherwise looked like a huge risk. He later shared,

> If we are to take risks, to be free, in the air, in life, we have to know there's a catcher. We have to know that when we come down from it all, we're going to be caught, we're going to be safe. The great hero is the least visible. Trust the catcher.[2]

I love that. Yes, faith requires that we take scary risks. But we can have the faith required because we have a God who is faithful.

Our Faithful God

When we put our faith in God, we find that he is faithful. When I say "put our faith in," I don't mean trusting in him for our salvation. That is true too. But in the Bible we see that faith always leads to action. In Hebrews 11 we find a list of faith heroes who have made it into God's "Faith Hall of Fame." The author of Hebrews introduces each figure with the phrase, "By faith, . . ." and then goes on to describe what the person did because of their faith. Faith led each of these heroes to action, and the action was

---

1. Henri J. M. Nouwen, *Sabbatical Journey: The Diary of His Final Year* (New York: Crossroad Publishing, 1998), 2.
2. Henri Nouwen, quoted in *Angels over the Net*, DVD, directed by The Company (New York: Spark Productions, 1995).

always risky. Faith moves us to go. In fact, James tells us, "Faith by itself, if it does not result in action, is dead" (James 2:17 BSB).

When we put our faith in God into action, when we move into outrageous obedience, we find that God is faithful. I think of so many examples.

Caleb and Joshua. Moses sent twelve of his men to spy out the land God had promised them. Read those last four words again. God had *already* promised them the land. But when the spies came back, ten announced there was no way they could ever possess the land. The people there were too big, too strong. Only Caleb and Joshua insisted that since God said he would give them the land, God *would* give them the land.

Because the people believed the ten men rather than God, because they weren't willing to go where God told them to go, they had to wander around in the wilderness until they withered away and died out there. But Caleb and Joshua lived through the loitering and entered the Promised Land. They put their faith in God and found that he was faithful.

George Müller. Born in Prussia in 1805, George Müller grew up stealing and lying and was so bad his parents sent him off to boarding school. In college, he was invited to a Bible study. Müller went, planning on making fun of those weak-minded people who believed in God. He ended up coming to faith. And coming to faith meant putting his faith into action.

Müller went into ministry, started a Bible college, distributed almost two million Bibles, and started many orphanages and one hundred seventeen schools. Then, at age seventy, he became a missionary. For the next seventeen years of his life, Müller traveled around the world sharing Jesus.

What blows me away is that he started all these ministries but never asked anyone for financial support. He had a personal conviction that he would only ask God for money and trust that God would lead his people to provide what was needed.

Müller wrote in his journal on June 15, 1837, "From the moment I asked until the Lord granted it fully, I never doubted that He would give every shilling of that sum. Often I praised Him in the assurance that He would grant my request."

The amount of money that came in to support Müller's ministry is astounding. One example: the finances God brought to the Bible college as an answer to prayer totaled about 1.5 million pounds. That was in the early 1800s. Today, that amount would be equal to about 180 million dollars. Müller put his faith in God and found that God was faithful.

Mother Antonia. There's a prison in Tijuana called La Mesa. In 2005, it was home to about six thousand of Mexico's worst criminals and one seventy-eight-year-old nun. Mother Antonia chose to make a tiny cell in the prison her home so that she could serve the prisoners. She spent her days praying and counseling hardened murderers, gang leaders, and drug lords. She also fought for their rights, making sure they had medicine and clean water. The prisoners loved her and called her Mother Antonia. She called them "my sons." The prison warden at the time, Francisco Jiminez, said of her, "Mother Antonia brings hope to men and women here. And they find hope themselves. She spreads the love of God."[3]

Mother Antonia moved into the prison in 1977. Before that, she was Mary Clarke, and she lived in Beverly Hills. Clarke sensed God's call to love the prisoners of La Mesa. Her faith overwhelmed her fear, and it led her to go.

Mother Antonia's love for the prisoners led to a dramatic transformation at La Mesa, though it continued to be a dangerous place. Once, when she wasn't there, a riot broke out. Mother Antonia returned to the prison that night and discovered soldiers surrounding it, doing their best to contain the violence. The prisoners had taken hostages, fires had broken out, bullets were flying. Mother Antonia told the police, "Let me go in; I know I can do something to stop the violence."[4]

They told her she couldn't go in because they feared for her safety. She explained:

> I'm not afraid. When you love, you don't have anything to be afraid of. Love casts out fear, the Bible tells us, and I love the men there. . . . I can go into the cells . . . see the men, pray for them, bring them hope. . . . That doesn't mean I'm in accord with them. That doesn't mean I'm not going to show them what's wrong and try to calm something down that's evil and wrong. It just doesn't stop me from loving them.[5]

3. Johnny Dodd, "From Beverly Hills to Mexican Jail," *People Magazine*, vol. 63, no. 20 (May 23, 2005), 97–98, https://www.johnnydodd.com/from-beverly-hills-to-a-mexican-jail/.

4. Matthew Lickona, "Mother Antonia Speaks," *San Diego Reader*, September 24, 2008, https://www.sandiegoreader.com/news/2008/sep/24/mother-antonia-speaks/.

5. Lickona, "Mother Antonia Speaks."

They relented and gave her permission to go in.

Mother Antonia walked into the prison and found an influential inmate named Blackie. She told him, "It's not right that you're locked up here, hungry and thirsty. We can take care of those things, but this isn't the way to do it. I will help you make it better. But first, you have to give me the guns. I beg you to put down your weapons." Blackie told her, "Mother, as soon as we heard your voice, we dropped the guns out the window."[6]

One pastor said of Mother Antonia, "She's a walking gift of love."[7] The truth is that Mother Antonia put her faith in God, and she found that God is faithful.

You? What about you? God wants *you* to be a walking gift of love, but it requires risk-taking faith. Where will your faith lead you? Who is God calling you to care for?

You might feel like you don't have enough faith, but Jesus said that if you have even a little faith, it can move mountains (see Matthew 17:20).

I believe that.

And I wonder what mountain is in the way of your outrageously obeying God. I wonder what stands in the way of your going where he has called you to go. What mountain do you need moved? Perhaps it's the mountain of fear. You might fear that you're not qualified for the task, or what the results will be, or rejection from others. It could be your mountain is a wound from past trauma that continues to keep you shackled. Or your mountain

---

6. Mary Jordan and Kevin Sullivan, *The Prison Angel: Mother Antonia's Journey from Beverly Hills to a Life of Service in a Mexican Jail* (New York: Penguin Books, 2005), ebook.

7. Dodd, "From Beverly Hills to Mexican Jail."

may be your comfort, your privilege, your apathy, or your wealth.

Do you believe God can move that mountain? He *can.* In fact, with just a little faith in the mighty name of Jesus, *you* can tell that mountain to move, and then you can move into your calling.

I know that probably scares you, but . . . trust the catcher. Trust the catcher and jump. If you do—if you put your faith in God—you'll find he is faithful.

Looking for a House

Remember how I was mortified and embarrassed and disappointed because purchasing the house fell through? I was angry at God for letting us down. We had raised seventy-five thousand dollars, which was just enough to buy the little run-down house and do some rehabbing.

Two months later, I got a call from one of our outreach volunteers. Chris told me she was walking through her church on Sunday morning and bumped into a woman she had not seen in years. The woman asked, "Hey, Chris, what have you been up to?" Chris laughed and said, "I've been hanging out with strippers." The woman was surprised, and Chris told her about our ministry. Out of nowhere, the woman asked, "Is that ministry looking for a house?" Chris shared the story of the fundraising gala and the house owner declining to sell. Then the woman made Chris an offer.

Chris called me and said, "This woman has a house for sale. Would you like to go see it?" I said no. Why? Because I knew we didn't have enough money. I knew seventy-five grand wasn't enough to buy a *real* house.

Chris didn't give up. She called me over and over, asking me to at least go look at the house. Each time I told her no. Buying a real house was not reasonable. I mean, I was already angry and disappointed; seeing a house we couldn't afford would just make me feel worse.

One day I was in a coffee shop with a couple of my board members when my phone rang. I didn't recognize the number but answered anyway. A woman's voice asked if I was Rachelle, and then she said that Chris had told her our ministry was looking for a house. She said, "We'd love for you to come by and look at this one." She gave me the address. It was one block from where I was sitting.

Okay. Fine.

I drove over. First, I saw the "For Sale" sign. Then, I saw the house. It was huge. It had to be more than twelve thousand square feet!

I started to drive away because I knew we could never afford a mansion like that, but there was a woman on the porch waving at me. *Ugh.*

The woman and her husband gave me a tour of the house. It was set up perfectly to be a transitional living home for women. They even told me that it was zoned exactly as we would need it to be.

After the tour, the husband asked, "What do you think?"

"It's beautiful." I frowned. "But we can't afford it."

He smiled at me and said, "No. We don't want to sell it to you. We want to give it to you!"

Wow. We wanted to buy a tiny, dilapidated house because it seemed reasonable. Our unreasonably faithful God gave us a mansion for free.

8

"Why Are You Running from God?"

Overcoming the Obstacles That Keep Us from Obedience

It was beautiful, and I hated it. We were staying in an amazing house on a cliff with a gorgeous view of the ocean. I was so angry about it I decided to run.

I told Josh I was going out. I stormed out of the house and started running the 1.3-mile Razor Point Trail.

My legs couldn't move quickly enough to keep up with my racing thoughts. My mind was overwhelmed with bitterness. *Here I am, running a trail I don't want to be on in a place I don't want to be.*

That's when *the* thought hit me. I heard God. And I realized that I need him in the exact same way the women in the sex industry need him. I wasn't only running a trail; I was running from God.

When We Won't Go

I met a woman once who told me, "I'm so glad you started Scarlet Hope. God called me to reach out to women in the sex industry forty years ago, but I just didn't know what to do."

I smiled and tried my best to be gracious, but forty years felt like an eternity. I was only thirty-two then. I thought about all the women and children who might have heard the gospel decades before if she'd had the courage to go. I wondered about her story and what her life must have been like to prevent her from going. Maybe she had young kids, maybe she had crippling anxiety, maybe she just got busy like the rest of us. . . . I don't know truly, but I couldn't shake the feeling that I'd met a modern-day Jonah.

You know the story. "The word of the LORD came to Jonah son of Amittai: 'Go to the great city of Nineveh and preach against it, because its wickedness has come up before me.' But Jonah ran away from the LORD" (Jonah 1:1–3). God called the prophet to go from Israel to what is now Iraq, and Jonah went in the opposite direction. He boarded a ship that was headed to Tarshish—across the Mediterranean to Spain.

We need to understand that the Israelites hated Nineveh. The Ninevites had besieged Israel's cities and starved the people. When violence between the nations broke out, Nineveh's leaders had been brutal, going so far as to impale Israelites on poles and leave them on the sides of the roads to celebrate their military victory.

It was this hatred of Ninevite sinners that kept Jonah from obedience. Can you imagine being a prophet in a post-war era and having God call you to cross enemy lines to witness to a people who had committed war crimes and mass murder against your own people?

God didn't tell Jonah to speak niceties to the heathen in Nineveh, but Jonah knew God's character. He knew it was God's will to seek and save sinners, not destroy them. And it would be just like God to lead the Ninevites to saving repentance. That is why he ran. His heart was set on a different outcome, one where he and his people would be vindicated and their enemies wiped out. Jonah found obedience too difficult because his heart was bent away from God's will.

We like to look down on Jonah, but I wonder if instead we should see ourselves in the runaway prophet. Sometimes we don't see ourselves in him because we think, *Jonah was running from God. I'm not. I love God.* But we forget that it's impossible to truly love God *and* run from his call.

Is that you? Is that me?

If so, I wonder why we run. Do you know?

The Fear Factor

Over the years, I have seen several ways people run away from obedience. Some run because of fear. We know God has called us to go to sinners—to seek and save the lost. And to go to sinners, you probably need to go to sinful places. But that scares us.

One way our fear reveals itself is in our keeping sinners and sinful places at a distance.

When we invite women to go into the clubs with us, some ask, "Why don't the people who work in the clubs just come to church?" Well, I do believe the church is God's Plan A for his mission in the world, but the church is not a building; it's a people. And God has called his church (his people) to go. He told us to go into the world to share his gospel with sinful people. We are to go, and then we can certainly bring the people we meet to church.

So, though it sounds nice when church people say, "They should come. We will love anyone who walks through our doors," I wonder if we say we want people to come because we don't want to go. We don't want our lives to be touched by the messiness of other people's sin.

We sit at home, order Uber Eats, and the closest we get to another person is giving a digital thumbs-up on a perfect handoff. Or maybe we feel frisky and walk into a coffee shop to order a coffee in person, *gasp*. But we have AirPods on to tune out the world and any chance of community.

Maybe we just don't go to the part of town where people are hurting because we know it's physically dangerous to be there. We keep sinners and sinful places at a distance so we can feel safe, and then we pray at night with our kids that God will keep us safe another day. We're putting our heads in the sand, hiding from realities that are breaking God's heart.

Most cities and towns in America are good at hiding the brokenness in the shadows. Our zoning codes and neighborhood associations keep the ugliness of poverty, addiction, and prostitution away from our front porches and driveways. The strip clubs are all located in a different part of town, and unless you live in Vegas or Atlantic City, it's not the part of town that gets celebrated. This is probably why people are so shocked when I share statistics about our city's adult entertainment industry or human trafficking in our state. They say they didn't know. But I think the truth is, we don't want to know.

Several years into the ministry of Scarlet Hope, we opened a bakery in one of the most dangerous parts of Louisville. Scarlet's Bakery was designed to work in tandem with our job-training program for women from the industry. It was a place where ladies who were leaving the clubs could learn the skills they needed to be on their own in the work force. We opened in that rougher part of town be-

We keep sinners and sinful places at a distance so we can feel safe, and then we pray at night with our kids that God will keep us safe another day. We're putting our heads in the sand, hiding from realities that are breaking God's heart.

cause it was close to a bus line, and it was also across the street from a local church.

We got a lot of Sunday morning worshipers who would come to eat treats and drink coffee. But the rest of the week, the bakery felt like a ghost town. Even if they loved the mission, most people didn't want to drive into a dangerous neighborhood. After all, you'd often bump into a homeless person right out front, or even inside.

It was easier for most folks to avoid the mess and the danger. They didn't want to know what was going on, because knowing would have been the first step in having to do something about it.

We're afraid to go because we'll know. Then, once we know, another wave of fear overwhelms us. We realize how messy and sordid the brokenness is, and we're tempted to think, *I can't. It's just too much. I wouldn't know what to say or to do. I can't change a person in that situation. I can't make a difference when the problems are that big.*

I get it. It's hard to understand someone whose struggles are different from your own. Whether it's someone from the clubs, a kid on drugs, or a woman in crisis who wants an abortion, the problems run deep, and there is a mountain of messiness.

But I have good news. It's not your job to know exactly what the person needs. God knows. It's not your job to save a person. Jesus does that. It's not your responsibility to change a person. The Holy Spirit is amazing at that. Your job is to love the person, to show them grace and patiently point them to Jesus. You can do that. But to do that, you will have to stop running. You'll have to go.

Comfortably Numb

Why do we run from obedience? For some, it's fear. But for others, it's a love of comfort that has led to complacency.

Again, I understand. I can get lured in by creature comforts. I love a good shopping spree, Starbucks pumpkin spice lattes, or getting my nails done. I think we can appreciate nice things, but not if our enjoyment of comfort leads us to complacency. The reality is that many aren't going because luxury has led them to apathy.

I have women express interest in serving with Scarlet Hope but then realize it doesn't look like what they thought it would. It's harder, messier, and more complex fitting it into everyday life. Often I hear, "My stage of life just can't fit this in right now." To some degree, I get that.

I'm a full-time wife, mom, daughter, sister, and friend as well. They tell me, "I want to come, but I'm just too busy to add more to my life right now." Business and comfort keep them from committing to the mission. It reminds me of the seed in Jesus's parable that falls "among the thorns," the person who "hears the word, but the worries of this life and the deceitfulness of wealth choke the word, making it unfruitful" (Matthew 13:22).

The reality is that many aren't going because luxury has led them to apathy.

We also see people who are like the seed that fell on rocky ground. They hear the Word and receive it with excitement, but "since they have no root, they last only a short time" (Matthew 13:21). It can be what my assistant, Emily, likes to call "next-shiny-object syndrome."

When Louie Giglio's Passion Conference highlighted sex trafficking, people came out of the woodwork to contact Scarlet Hope. We had fifty people sign up to serve in our ministry, but maybe five stuck it out. Most of the women who came to us responded emotionally to the stories told at the conference, but they didn't understand what serving in our ministry would involve. These women were attracted to a ministry that seemed exciting, but their love waned when the wrinkles and blemishes of difficult work were exposed. They moved on the moment they discovered that ministry is messy.

Some run because of fears and others because of comfort, but I believe the biggest reason people run from obedience is judgment. Because we're just like Jonah.

Seek and ~~Save~~ JUDGE the Lost

It was a beautiful Sunday morning. I woke up early, pumped to pick up a new friend I'd met at the club to bring her to church. She—we'll call her Erin—was excited too. We'd visited Erin's club the Thursday night before, and as I walked in, I saw her eagerly waiting for us.

"Will you take me to church?" she asked.

I. Couldn't. Believe. It.

"Of course! I'll definitely take you to church."

We'd only been in the club a few short months, and God was already answering prayers. Because I love the church, my desire from the beginning of our ministry was to connect women in the adult entertainment industry to Christ's body. I want them to experience Christian community and be built up and encouraged by worship and Bible teaching.

That Sunday morning, I got up and drove out into the country where Erin lived. I knocked on the door of a house with weeds growing up all around it. The front door was broken, and inside it looked dark and scary. I'd met women under the dark lights of the clubs, but this was one of the first times I'd been to a dancer's house. I discovered that dancers are under darkness when they're away from the clubs as well.

I knocked and waited. Then knocked and waited. It felt like forever, but I stayed and prayed at the door. Finally, it opened, and a drowsy Erin stood before me. She had black and blue bruises all over her legs, arms, and face. Under the black lights, I had not seen this reality.

"Do you still want to go to church?" I asked.

"Yeah, sorry," she said, "I got home from the club at 4 a.m. and I overslept my alarm."

Erin gathered herself, got dressed, threw on a coat, and we headed out. I didn't look at what she was wearing. Honestly, I didn't care. It was an act of God that she'd gotten out of her bed after such a late night. I was just happy she'd committed to going to a church service with me.

During our visits to the club, Erin had shared that her family and friends warned her about church, saying, "If you ever set foot in a church building, the whole place will collapse." Erin had listened to them. She'd never been to church in her entire life.

When we got to the church parking lot, Erin grabbed my arm and held it tight. I think she was nervous and required extra support to take those steps we all find so easy every Sunday. We walked in and she took off her coat. That's when I finally looked at what she was wearing. She had on tight white jeans, some of her dancer high heels, and a bright purple top with the B word spelled out in shiny sequins across the front. I had to laugh. I thought, *Okay, God, you're right, this is exactly who you call. There's no shirt or shoes that will stop you from rescuing your daughters.*

I led Erin into the church service, and she was engaged in every moment of it. She listened to the sermon and cried from the beginning to the end. God spoke to her. Erin was recognizing Christ's love for the first time in her life.

After the service, as we headed for the door, one of the church's elders pulled me aside. He knew about our new ministry to the clubs, but he was obviously offended by Erin's outfit. He spoke to me sternly. "Rachelle, I know you want to bring these women to church, but you can't bring them here looking like that!"

My heart sank. I stood there astonished at his words. Frankly, I was angry. I finally understood what the women in the clubs meant when they'd tell me I was weird. That they'd seen the church signs that say "Come as you are" but had never met a Christian who truly loved them "as they are" without first requiring they get cleaned up and meet certain cultural expectations.

I learned something when I went to church with Erin that day. Of all the obstacles that stand in the way of risk-taking, courageous faith, the biggest is in our own hearts. Too many hearts are filled with judgment for sinners rather than love. Too often it is Christians who are standing in the way of the very people Jesus is calling to himself.

What's amazing to me is that Christians seem to feel justified in judging sinners. That blows my mind because, well, where do we see Jesus judging sinners? Where do we see him pointing an accusing finger at people trapped in their sin? Nowhere. The only people we see Jesus condemning were the Pharisees . . . because they condemned sinners. The only people to whom Jesus didn't show grace were people who claimed to represent God but withheld his grace from others. Jesus loved sinners no matter who they were, what they had done, or how they might respond. He told the Pharisees, "It is not the healthy who need a doctor, but the sick" (Matthew 9:12).

It's ironic; I think the elder that Sunday morning felt like he was protecting his church from sin, but what he was really doing was preventing his church from living out their mission to sinners. In the guise of holiness, he was running from God's mission and leading his church to do the same.

I'll be honest. I hate judgment, but sometimes I am tempted to judge Christians who are running from God. Then that day came when I realized that *I* was running from God.

The Leader Who Wouldn't Stop

When I heard God call me to reach women in the adult entertainment industry, I didn't run away like Jonah; I pressed in. Josh tells me I'm just wired to be the *Go* girl. (He means that as a positive, but my personality can also be a problem.)

It took a while for me to see that, but after nearly a decade of being immersed in the ministry of Scarlet Hope, Josh began to tell me to slow down. In fact, everyone was asking me to slow down. One day I found my assistant, Emily, sitting on the steps of our ministry office, crying. She begged me, "You can't keep the pace you have. You can't— even subconsciously—keep making all of us on staff keep up with you. Can we please take a time out?"

I wouldn't do it. I couldn't take my foot off the accelerator.

In 2014, I put together a four-part strategic plan. Our board chairman, a friend named Bryce Butler, helped me present it to the Scarlet Hope board. It was a huge vision— opening a day program for women, starting the bakery, collaborating with similar ministries around the country, and ministering to *every* woman in the adult entertainment industry in Louisville. This big plan was supposed to take five years. We accomplished it in one.

We had a newly adopted one-year-old at home, and Josh kept saying, "Please slow down. You have a kid now." Bryce, who had taught me a lot about entrepreneurship, approached me and said, "We can't keep going at this rate. We can't keep burning the candle at both ends." I nodded but thought, *No. I don't care what these people say! We have to GO.*

Then came the end of 2016. That's when the board stopped me in my tracks by sending me on a four-month sabbatical. The board asked me to make myself as unavailable as possible. I couldn't call staff or talk to anyone in the ministry, and I didn't have access to my everyday life. Instead, I was seeing a counselor during that time, Rich Plass of Crosspoint Ministries.

During the sabbatical, Rich kept asking me a question: "Why are you running from God?"

What?

I remember looking at Rich and thinking, *Are you kidding me? I'm not going to answer that stupid question. Why on earth would you ask me that? That's not what I'm doing. That's the kind of thing women who hear God's voice and then sit on their butts for forty years do.*

Rich is an older, wiser man and a stoic counselor. I refused to answer his question, but he wouldn't budge. "That's the question I'm asking you. That's your directive. You've got to answer that question."

During the four months away from work, Josh and I traveled to Del Mar, California. We got to stay in an incredible house on a cliff with a breathtaking view of the ocean. As I mentioned, it was gorgeous and relaxing, and I hated it. I'd have phone calls with Rich and ask, "Why am I even doing this? I don't want to be here. I want to be back in Kentucky. I need to be leading my ministry." Rich would listen to me whine and then ask, "Rachelle, why are you running from God?"

I'm the sort of person who despises exercise, but one day I was bored out of my mind and needed to get out of my luxurious prison, so I looked at Josh and told him, "I'm going for a run."

"Where are you going?"

"To Torrey Pines."

I headed up the 1.3-mile Razor Point Trail through the park's dramatic views of ravines and badlands. For much of the run, the desert is on one side and ocean cliffs are on the other.

I laugh about it now, but I was listening to the pop song "The Mack" by Nevada over and over. I was really worked up inside. I kept pushing forward, and it was like every step was driven by resentment toward all the people who were trying to slow me down.

At one point, I was trekking up the path when I looked down and saw a huge cactus with large spines. In that moment, I sensed the Holy Spirit say, "My thorns were for you."

Whoa.

It hit me. I'd been telling women from the industry that God's love is for them, but I'd somehow forgotten that it was also for me. I taught others that it's Christ's love that compels us. We know we are loved by Jesus, and we go because of that love. But that's *not* the way I was living. I didn't *really* believe God loved *me* with perfect love and compassion. I was trying to earn his love and had started to root my identity in my calling rather than in the one who called me.

That's why I was unwilling to slow down, even for a day or a temporary sabbatical. I was always running. And for the first time, I realized my counselor was right. I was running from God.

Shauna Niequist described my problem perfectly in her book *Present Over Perfect* when she wrote, "I can't hear the voice of love when I'm hustling. All I can hear are my own feet pounding the pavement."[1] Instead of sitting still and silent and dealing with the empty space inside—instead of leaving room to *know* I was the beloved daughter of my Father—I was running in hopes of earning his approval and love.

I stopped running and just stood there in that spot on the trail for hours, soaking in the moment.

It was a turning point for me. For years I had felt a burden that if I didn't do the job I'm called to do, women would die and go to hell. Frankly, the urgency that women are lost and far from God still drives me. But at the same time, I've had to learn to live in light of different realities. Whether I do my job or not, I am still loved. And God loves the women I am called to reach more than I do. Ultimately, God is the one who does the saving work. I'm not the Savior. No, I *need* the Savior. And the only way for both me and our Scarlet Hope teams to participate in the saving work God is already doing is to remember how desperate we are for his love every day.

When I came back to the ministry in March of 2017, I was finally able to embrace my limitations. I began to see

1. Shauna Niequist, *Present Over Perfect: Leaving Behind Frantic for a Simpler, More Soulful Way of Living* (Grand Rapids, MI: Zondervan, 2016), 27.

that I'd lost the clear sense of the specific work to which God had called me. I'd started piling on lots of other responsibilities I wasn't gifted or skilled to do. It was killing me and the people around me. I told our board, "Here is the stuff I'm not good at. Here's what's hurting me and the ministry." Bryce smiled and told me, "We've just been waiting for you to see it."

Why Are *You* Running from God?

There are obstacles to obedience for every Christian. It doesn't matter whether you've been doing ministry for years or if you're that woman who is waiting until you aren't so busy, or until all the pieces of the puzzle seem to fit.

I think the first step toward going is understanding why you've been staying.

Are you afraid? Maybe courageous, risk-taking faith doesn't come naturally to you or isn't something your church has ever encouraged. Nevertheless, you can overcome your fear because God promises he'll go with you.

Are you complacent and comfortable? There is a woman in our ministry named Ronelle. Four years ago, she retired from a big corporate job in our city to serve with our ministry. Every day since she's dropped whatever she's doing to serve whenever we need her. What leads her to live like that?

In Revelation, there's a short description of the martyrs who have given their lives for the faith. It says, "They did not love their lives so much as to shrink from death" (Revelation 12:11). Ronelle doesn't love her life so much as to shrink back from what's difficult. You know what the difference is between you and Ronelle? Nothing. She broke out of her comfortable complacency and dove into outrageous obedience. What she has done, you can do.

Have you been running so hard you've forgotten your first love? On sabbatical, I didn't lose my passion, but I did learn to rest. I learned to rest *in* the work to which God had called me. I stopped running, and I obeyed the Spirit's voice that had been speaking through the people around me. I came back from sabbatical a different Rachelle. I passed on the leadership of the local Scarlet Hope ministry to Ronelle, and I now focus my work on the expansion of our network of ministries. I learned to rest in the reality that his thorns are for me.

You can experience that kind of rest too. It's not a rest from work; it's a rest in your work for the Lord. Rest *from* would be an obstacle to obedience. No, God gives us rest *in*; a rest in our souls—rest in his compassion, grace, and love—and that rest will give you the confidence to obey him. That rest fuels you to serve and love others and to stay within the limits of your unique gifting.

> **God gives us rest *in*; a rest in our souls—rest in his compassion, grace, and love—and that rest will give you the confidence to obey him.**

Your story so far may be about running, but I believe God is going to make it a story of grace-motivated obedience. That's what God did with Jonah. When Jonah ran, God sent uncomfortable grace—a storm and a great fish. When the prophet prayed, God in his grace drew near and rescued him. When Jonah preached, God's grace changed the Ninevites. And when he got angry and complained about God's grace poured out toward sinners, God sent a leafy vine to gently correct him. Jonah tried to run, but as Paul David Tripp says, "You can't outrun grace."[2]

You might be like the woman I met who felt called forty years ago. Well, God has been patiently pursuing you. The Holy Spirit is chasing you down. Let him catch you. Stop running from God and start going in obedience to him.

2. Paul David Tripp, *Jonah: You Can't Outrun Grace* (The Hub, 2017).

9

"Where You Go, I'll Go Too."

Bringing Others Along

God has put a calling on your life. You sense it. You feel it. You're excited but also intimidated. You want to go, but you may feel like you first must get through a maze of questions. You might be asking:

Do I have what it takes?
What if the needs are greater than I can handle?
What if this requires gifts or expertise I don't have?
What about when it gets difficult?

Those are real questions. In fact, they stop a lot of people from answering God's call.

And depending on your calling, the questions may be even more daunting. As I've said, not everyone is called to go into the strip clubs. You might be called to take care of your aging parent or to come alongside a single mom and help with her kids in a significant way. But if God has called you to follow him into a dark place, you probably feel overwhelmed by other questions.

What if I can't find my way?
What if the darkness overwhelms me?

You need to go. Even with unanswered questions, you need to go. That's what faith is for—it gives us confidence and assurance even when we cannot see all the answers (see Hebrews 11:1).

God has called you to go—even without all the answers—but, good news, he's got an answer for all those questions.

I know because I've experienced it.

Can I Go with You?

When God first spoke to me driving past that strip club on my way to work, I happened to be meeting weekly with my friend Sarah at our local Panera. We were working through Kelly Minter's Bible study on the book of Ruth, and we'd been talking about how God was calling me to go and share his hope and love with women in the adult entertainment industry.

Then one day—like Ruth said to Naomi—Sarah looked me in the eyes and told me, "Where you go, I'll go too. I don't think you can do this alone."

You can't imagine the confidence those words gave me. I heard that and knew I could keep going forward. I realized

I wasn't going to reach women in the clubs by myself, and now knew I wouldn't be alone.

Not long after that, Sarah and I started driving around Louisville strip clubs each Tuesday night in my little red Focus. We prayed God would open a door and show us the way to minister to the women inside. Our husbands went with us most of the time. Looking back, I guess they were scared for us. Though we were just praying in our cars, we were in some shady places in town, so they wanted to be there for protection.

When our husbands couldn't come, Sarah and I would sit inside the Wendy's across from the Fantasy X club and pray for the people we saw headed inside. We met off and on for over a year to drive past clubs or to just sit and pray.

Scarlet Hope began with the four of us—me, my husband, Sarah, and her husband—but over time others came along too. In those beginning stages when we were doing the prayer drives, I would tell people about the vision for our ministry, and they'd share it with others. Pretty soon, people started asking, "Hey, can I go with you?"

Then the day came when we entered the clubs for the first time. When we had moved to Indiana for Josh to work at the church, he took a big pay cut. So I started a little side-hustle catering company to help make ends meet. When the Lord told me to go into the clubs, the idea of serving meals to the women there seemed natural. I already knew how to cook and serve a lot of people, but catering takes a team. So it was essential for Sarah and me to gather other women who would help us cook and go into the clubs with us to serve the food.

In those beginning days of our ministry, Sarah made cookies at her house, and someone else would bake and bring bread. It's crazy now to think that this strip club would allow us to bring a home-cooked meal into their business, but they did. God prepared the way for us, and preparing those meals together was the way he grew our ministry. He brought woman after woman to join us.

It wasn't just women who made our ministry possible. Two key figures in those early days were pastors—Chris Harper and Travis Whalen. They supported the work, prayed for us, and spurred us on. Chris was the missions director at our church and one of our first financial supporters. I think we were six months into the ministry and didn't even yet have a name when he wrote us into the church mission budget.

Chris had heard about what we were doing and asked me, "How much money do you need?"

I had no idea. I blurted out, "Umm, a hundred dollars per month?"

Chris fired right back, "Great, I'll put it in the budget." And he did. What an affirmation that was. It was the Lord assuring me, through his people, "I'm going to provide. I'm going to do this. You don't have to worry."

God is always with us. That's something I clung to from Jesus's command in Matthew. I trusted that he was all sufficient. Because of that, I think sometimes we look only to him. But sometimes the answer God provides to all those questions that slow us down is *friends*. In the beginning, God said it was not good for man to be alone, and that's still true today. The stakes are even higher when you're responding to God's call and following him into the dark. You need people who will go with you.

In life and ministry, we need friends like Sarah and Chris. We need a supportive community that partners with us and helps us carry the mission forward. As the old African proverb says, "If you want to go fast, go alone. But if you want to go far, *go together.*"

Friends on Mission Together

True friendship is locking arms and walking beside one another with one heart and one mission. In his chapter on friendship in *The Four Loves*, C. S. Lewis says friendship always arises from a common interest. "It may be a common religion, common studies, a common profession, even a common recreation. All who share it will be our companions."[1] I love that. At Scarlet Hope, we have a common *purpose*. It's not merely to get women out of the adult entertainment industry. Our mission is to help those women know Jesus. And when you're on that same mission together, you build strong connections.

Believe this truth: real friends go on mission together. Their friendship is built around a common commitment to a shared purpose.

At Scarlet Hope, we want to build deep relationships within our team and with the people we're serving. Sometimes when people talk to me about volunteering in our ministry, they ask, "How long do I have to serve?" Usually I answer, "I'd like you to commit for a year. After all, you're only seeing the women in

> **Real friends go on mission together. Their friendship is built around a common commitment to a shared purpose.**

1. C. S. Lewis, *The Four Loves* (New York: Harcourt, Brace and Company, 1960), 97.

the clubs a few times each month. So how can you build a relationship of trust with someone if you're only seeing her a couple times each month and stop in less than a year?"

Some folks are taken aback: "A year?"

Now, we're obviously not going to force anyone to serve with us forever, but I tell them, "Yeah, a year." I mean, if you're looking for a one-and-done service opportunity, then go to a soup kitchen. Or maybe don't even go there. The truth is that those who minister to the homeless are also looking for people who will walk arm in arm with them toward a common goal.

Too often, people want to serve with us *once*. They've heard our incredible stories and want to be a part of one. Our human hearts want to see immediate fruit, and we may hesitate to commit for the long haul. Immediate fruit is rare, if not almost impossible. But over time, a community of friends can build something amazing. Many of the people who serve in our ministry today benefit from the longevity of those who have served much longer. Our teams in Louisville can now go to pretty much any strip club in the city, but that's because a group of friends invested fourteen years of hard work serving and helping the women in the clubs.

When you're going into the dark, you cannot go by yourself. You must have people there with you. We're not meant to go it alone. Not even Jesus did. He had twelve disciples—three who were very close confidants. And when Jesus sent out his disciples, he sent them two-by-two so they could share encouragement and accountability. If we're going to be on mission today, we've got to follow his example. We're supposed to partner together with others in the kingdom work.

I'm convinced if you commit to go with God, he'll provide someone to go with you.

"Your God Will Be My God"

Think back with me to the story of Ruth. Ruth's friendship and commitment to Naomi were born out of great loss. During the time of the judges, there was a great famine in Israel. So Naomi's husband, Elimelek, left Bethlehem in Judah and took her and their two sons, Mahlon and Kilion, away from God's community to the land of Moab (see Ruth 1:1–2).

While they were in Moabite territory, Elimelek died. Then Mahlon and Kilion each married a Moabite woman. One was named Orpah and the other Ruth. The Bible tells us, "After they had lived there about ten years, both Mahlon and Kilion also died, and Naomi was left without her two sons and her husband" (Ruth 1:4–5).

Naomi was left destitute. There was no way for a widow to support herself in that ancient society. And to add insult to injury, this wasn't even Naomi's society. She was living as an exile in a foreign land. And Naomi was not just suffering financial loss, she was also grieving the loss of her husband and two sons. Later, she told Ruth to call her *Mara*, which means "bitter," because "the LORD has afflicted me; the Almighty has brought misfortune upon me" (Ruth 1:20–21). I've been in some pretty low places, but never so bad I've wanted to change my name to Bitter.

But just when it seems like this story might conclude with loss and sadness, Naomi hears that God came to the aid of his people by providing food for them. So she packed up her few belongings and set out with her two daughters-in-law on the road that would take them back to Judah (Ruth 1:6–7).

Then, as they neared the edge of the Israelite territory, Naomi said to her daughters-in-law, "Go back, each of you, to your mother's home. May the LORD show you kindness, as you have shown kindness to your dead husbands and to me. May the LORD grant that each of you will find rest in the home of another husband" (Ruth 1:8–9).

Orpah turned back and went home to Moab. But Ruth replied, "Don't urge me to leave you or to turn back from you. Where you go I will go, and where you stay I will stay. Your people will be my people and your God my God" (Ruth 1:16).

Faithfulness to the God of Israel was Ruth and Naomi's common commitment. He kept them walking side by side. Naomi could have been consumed by the darkness of grief if not for the one who stayed with her. Honestly, I think our human tendency is to keep at a distance those who are experiencing deep darkness. But the beautiful thing about this story is that Naomi and Ruth keep moving toward community. Ruth moves toward her mother-in-law. They both move back to Israel and God's people. And in their faithfulness, they're moving toward God even though he probably seemed far away.

> Our human tendency is to keep at a distance those who are experiencing deep darkness. But the beautiful thing about this story is that Naomi and Ruth keep moving toward community.

I've talked to a lot of people who have said, "I can't serve the Lord or volunteer in Scarlet Hope, because . . ." and then they describe something bad they've done or, more often, something painful that's happened to them. I never know how to respond. I want to be sensitive, but I know God is still calling this person to go. I mean, how do you answer someone whose response to pain has been to turn inward and introspective? How do you encourage someone whose hurt has kept them from going? I want so bad to shout, "This is your chance to find purpose in your pain and make a difference in the lives of others!"

Recently I met with a friend who came over to talk to me about what was on her heart. She shared with me that she has spent her whole life in church. She's gotten married and raised kids. Now she's fifty and has no idea what the purpose of her life is or how to be used by God.

She told me, "I've done every Bible study with a group of women for almost thirty years. We have had great times together learning about the Lord, but, well, I have this urging in my spirit to go. But I just don't know where to go."

I asked if she felt like she had a particular burden or area that her heart moved for.

She said, "No—that's what I need your help finding."

I was instantly reminded of this quote in *Experiencing God.*

Many people want God to call them to a big assignment. However, they try to bypass the love relationship . . . the love relationship is why God created you. That is far more important to Him than what you do. So anticipate that God will start working with you and drawing you to an intimate love relationship that is real and personal. When the love relationship is right, God will be free to begin giving you assignments at His initiative. Whenever you do not seem to be receiving assignments from God, focus on the love relationship and stay there until the assignment comes.[2]

So I encouraged her that as she continues to fall in love with the Lord, he will equip her for his calling.

Think back to the story of Ruth. Ruth had absolutely nothing. She and Naomi didn't even have food to eat. She became one of the poor wanderers in Israel, walking behind the people in the fields collecting any leftover sheaves of wheat. And yet Ruth found joy—and preservation—because she wasn't thinking about herself. She had locked arms with Naomi and was following Naomi's God.

Can you imagine locking arms with a bitter widow? Nobody wants to be around a bitter woman, but Ruth graciously drew near and said, "I'll go where you go; I'll die where you die." Why? Because Naomi's God was her God. And Boaz noticed the way Ruth loved God and Naomi. (I'm sure he noticed other things too. He was a man, after all.) But the Bible tells us that he noticed her love for the Lord and her care for her mother-in-law. And here's the thing: The Lord healed Naomi's bitterness as a result. As these two women locked arms and moved toward the Lord together, God redeemed them and wove them into his grand story.

I believe he wants to do the same for you.

Here are some things that helped me while I waited on the Lord to answer my prayer and give me a purpose.

2. Blackaby, *Experiencing God*, 121.

1. I think the most important thing you can do to find your calling is to pray and seek the Lord through prayer and fasting. Ask God to humble your heart and make it ready for his voice.

2. Spend time in silence listening to the Lord. Far too often we don't sit long enough in quiet to hear his voice clearly.

3. Learn what Jesus did when he was here on this earth. Who did he hang out with? How did he trust the Father with each and every person the Father put in his path?

4. God's timeline is not our own. I was diligently seeking his voice for two years before he spoke. Perseverance and patience in the waiting are challenging, but God promises to speak to those he is calling.

Stronger Together: Every Gifted Person Playing Their Part

The Scarlet Hope story is one of God unleashing the gospel to women who are usually ignored and despised by the church. But the call to reach women in the adult entertainment industry is bigger than me and our ministry in Louisville. After our ministry had been going for a few years, people heard what we were doing and started contacting us. "I've heard about you," they'd say. "We want to do that too. Can you train us?"

We were surprised but answered, "Yes!" and held our first strip club outreach training in 2009. That was the same year we became a federally recognized nonprofit. So from the very beginning we've had opportunities to partner and collaborate with like-minded women. Now through the Scarlet Hope Network, we support Scarlet Hope ministries in other cities, including Cincinnati, Reno, Las Vegas, Nashville, Miami, and Denver. Most of these ministries were started organically by ladies who served with us in Louisville and then moved to a new city and wanted to initiate the same kind of work there.

The goal of the network is to resource local ministries so the women leading them can focus on serving women on the streets, in their local strip clubs or massage parlors, and anywhere a woman is being exploited and trafficked. With the recently launched Scarlet Hope ministry in Miami, we were able to give the leaders fourteen years and millions of dollars' worth of developed resources—a ministry in a box, you might say.

We also have regular trainings and hold retreats for leaders in this ministry. The training isn't just for those who are part of the Scarlet Hope Network. We've trained women all over the world, from Romania to Costa Rica, to share the hope and love of Jesus with women in the adult entertainment industry. The grand and joyful story of God saving women in the clubs has gripped a whole community of women who now lock arms and collaborate.

Sadly, it's not always this way. I know of one city where five organizations are seeking to work with women in the industry, but none want to partner together. These divided believers are constantly fighting, and it looks confusing to the people in the clubs who they're trying to serve.

The apostle Paul encountered the same thing in the city of Corinth. The church was divided. Some were saying,

"I follow Apollos" and others, "I follow Paul" (see 1 Corinthians 3:4). Paul's answer was, "Get your eyes off yourself and your silly factions. We're on the same team. This is God's mission, and everyone's got a part to play."

In ministry, each of us has different gifts and serves a different purpose at different times. The results also vary. Sometimes our fruit grows on other people's trees. I think that's so cool. I may have gone into a strip club for four years straight, seen the same girls, and built great relationships with them, but I won't necessarily see the fruit of them coming to know Jesus. No doubt God used me, but the mission is not about me. There have been times when I've planted the seeds and then a new volunteer comes on who connects immediately with a woman in a different way, and as a result, the woman quickly comes to know the Lord. It's just a reminder to me that in our work together, God is the one doing the work through us. As Paul told the infighting Corinthians: "I planted the seed, Apollos watered it, but God has been making it grow. So neither the one who plants nor the one who waters is anything, but only God . . . For we are co-workers in God's service" (1 Corinthians 3:6–9).

We are coworkers in God's harvest field, and each gifted person is used by God in different ways for different people. Gifted members of a local church need one another and must partner together. A local Scarlet Hope ministry can't do everything either. We focus on serving women in the clubs and providing career development and employment. But to provide holistic care for these women, there's a need to partner with other organizations that provide services Scarlet Hope doesn't, such as ministries that offer housing, rehab and care for addiction, and gospel-centered, trauma-informed counseling.

Scarlet Hope would never have made it and would not be doing what we do today without a community of support. The same is true for you. You need a friend, or perhaps a few friends, who will lock arms and walk with you.

If you've heard God's call and stepped out in obedience, the next step is to share your joy with others. Remember how women joined my ministry when it was just a vision from God and not really a ministry at all. Start sharing what God has put on your heart with faithful women. They're not all going to join you—God has given us each different passions—but one will. Perhaps more than one.

> We are coworkers in God's harvest field, and each gifted person is used by God in different ways for different people.

Explain why you're doing what you're doing, why you're passionate about it, and invite them to come along. When you do, you multiply your impact. It's true because of God's design. He's chosen to move his mission forward through people who partner together.

10

"Can We Sing a Song?"

The Mission Moves Forward
as We Walk by the Spirit

Broken lightbulbs circled the cracked dressing room mirrors. The few working bulbs barely lit the cramped space enough to see the graffiti- and gum-tattooed lockers. A thick layer of grime covered most of the carpet. The room was cramped, space enough for four but filled with ten to twelve women on the nights when our volunteers joined the dancers.

Who would have thought this would be where we'd experience a holy moment?

Did I mention the whole club was small? I didn't, but it was. A bar on the left, a little stage on the right, a few tables and chairs in between. There was only one door to the stage. Our team would go up there and file through that door to carry all the food and serving dishes to the little dimly lit, broken-bulb dressing area.

We'd set up the weekly meal at the makeup bar, which had only two or three seats. Joy was always sitting in one of those seats. She was a bubbly woman who didn't know a stranger. She had been in the clubs for most of her life but seemed out of place. The first time we met Joy, she told us why right away.

"I sing in the choir in my church," Joy offered unprompted.

"Wow, that's crazy. What kind of church are we talking about here?"

"It's the little bitty Baptist church where my grandparents took me when I was growing up."

There it was. Here was a girl who belonged to Jesus—a daughter of the King! But we found her in the most unlikely place. *What is this girl doing? She loves Jesus. Why is she here?*

Throughout the night we would serve the women a meal and then post up in the dressing room to chat with them since that was always a better place to visit with them than the dance floor. These ladies would be in and out of the crowded dressing room for our entire visit.

But Joy would come back to the dressing room, sit there, talk, and cry. We graciously asked Joy why she was involved at her church during the day but stripping in the club at night. Then we learned Joy's story—her trauma and abuse.

Joy's mother had worked in the clubs too, and her dad wasn't in the picture. She'd lived in poverty for most of her life. Joy told us she'd found herself in this lifestyle, didn't want to be in it anymore, but didn't know how to leave. Listening to her, I realized the Holy Spirit was already working in her life to convict and encourage her. Joy's faith was weak and confused, but she was still a daughter of the King, and God had sent us to her.

Who is God sending *you* to? People who are hurting or lost spiritually or whose faith is faltering. It may not be in a strip club. God may be directing you to your neighbor's house, a park where the homeless hang out, a crisis pregnancy center, or a teen center in a housing project. I don't know where God is leading you, but I do know wherever it is, he is already there and already working.

Finding God at Work in the Strangest Places

In chapter 5, I quoted Henry Blackaby's maxim that "God is always at work around you." It's true. He's always working! And our eyes need to be open, looking for what he's doing. It's amazing to me that God was at work in that tiny strip club before we even arrived there.

Jesus found his Father at work in strange places too. In John 4, Jesus traveled through Samaria to a town called Sychar (John 4:4–5). The Jewish people despised Samaritans because they had intermarried with the Assyrians (see 2 Kings 17:24–31) and followed what the Jews regarded as pagan worship practices (see John 8:48; Luke 10:33). Most Jews would not even enter Samaria. When Jesus led his disciples there, they were probably confused and wanted to hurry through as quickly as possible. But Jesus knew God was at work even among those who were socially despised and regarded as ethnic half-breeds.

Jesus stopped in Sychar at Jacob's well. There he met an uneducated and immoral woman and asked her for a drink. This was an incredible breach of social customs.

Watering holes are famous as places where men go to pick up women. It's been true since the beginning of time (see Genesis 24:12–27; 29:9–12).

The woman had to wonder what Jesus was really looking for. She said to him, "You are a Jew and I am a Samaritan woman. How can you ask me for a drink?" (John 4:9).

Jesus responded, "If you knew the gift of God and who it is that asks you for a drink, you would have asked him and he would have given you living water" (John 4:10).

Jesus answered her cryptically, but he was aware of the great plan his Father has for his daughters. As the conversation continued, he told her how he had come to satisfy her deepest longing for eternal life (John 4:14). He gently confronted her failures and sins (John 4:16–18), and he promised her a day was coming when true worshipers would worship the Father in Spirit and in truth (John 4:21–24).

Finally, Jesus revealed himself to this woman as the Messiah, and the woman immediately began to *GO*. She left her water jar at the well, ran into the village, and said to the people, "Come, see a man who told me everything I ever did. Could this be the Messiah?" (John 4:29).

Relying on the Spirit

Do you assume God is already at work in the people and places you might least expect?

When you're not sure you can do what God is calling you to do, does it embolden you to know you're not alone? If you are following Jesus, he is with you, and he can make the impossible possible.

When you're having a spiritual conversation with someone who needs Jesus and anxiety starts to rise, do you realize God has already been speaking to that person?

When you're about to venture into the dark to do ministry, does it calm you to know God is already in that place?

Understanding that God is already working and is with you changes everything.

I've told you that when you head into the clubs, you must be sensitive to the Holy Spirit. In those moments when I'm ministering in a dark and dingy dressing room, I am intensely aware of how desperate I am for God's help. Yes, I need the Spirit every second of every day. But in the clubs, I am constantly praying. In my spirit, I'll say, *Jesus, give me words to speak to this woman. Give me wisdom for how to interact with this manager. Help the awkwardness our team feels to not show on our faces. Help us to show your love instead.*

Do you assume God is already at work in the people and places you might least expect? . . . Understanding that God is already working and is with you changes everything.

We encourage every volunteer in our ministry to have this prayerful mindset. When we're training women to go out to the clubs, we explain, "You are the missionary. And you are not merely going behind Scarlet Hope's name, you are going with the Lord. He is with you as you go into the clubs." We encourage our new volunteers to consult God on every decision. For instance, "When the night is getting long and you're wondering whether you should stay or go, ask God. You might pray, 'Holy Spirit, should we stay here longer? Is there someone else you want me to talk to?'"

I could give you thousands of stories of times when the Holy Spirit spoke to our team and said, "Wait." And then, in a beautiful, God-ordained moment, a woman would come up and share her heart with us, ask for help, or express a desire to give her life to the Lord.

In his book *Forgotten God*, Francis Chan unpacks a theology of the Holy Spirit. Chan writes,

> While some of the [theological] debates and conversations that take place are peripheral and don't have to be definitively resolved in order for us to live a faithful life, many theological issues are not this way. Some theological issues are absolutely vital to our faith. These are the ones where what we believe determines how we act.[1]

I love that quote because Chan makes the connection between what we *believe* about the third person of the Trinity and what we *do* with what we believe. We can believe God speaks to us and guides us through his Spirit, but do we listen, and will we obey?

Sometimes our volunteers bring up a very practical question about the Holy Spirit. They'll ask, "How do you know what the Spirit is saying?" You may have wondered the same thing.

Five big theological truths help us answer that question.
First, the Spirit is consistent with his messaging. The Holy Spirit's voice never says anything contrary to God's revealed Word. In fact, the Bible teaches us that one of the Spirit's jobs is to remind us of the things we've learned from God's

1. Francis Chan, *Forgotten God: Reversing Our Tragic Neglect of the Holy Spirit* (Colorado Springs, CO: David C. Cook, 2009), 64–65.

Word (John 16:13). For example, the Holy Spirit is never going to tell you to hurt or gossip about someone, right? No, he's going to prompt you to confess your sins, obey him, show love to someone who is difficult, or stop talking and listen to a friend who's in pain. What he tells you will always agree with what God has already told you in the Bible.

Second, the Spirit can't be manipulated. Some Christians think the Holy Spirit can be conjured up by how loudly you sing or how much you jump around. This is reinforced when people are really feeling an emotional high during a worship song and the pastor says, "Do you feel the Spirit?"

I've been in six-hour prayer meetings where it felt like the leaders thought if you prayed long enough, the Holy Spirit would have no choice but to show up. But truthfully, the Spirit is already there. We don't have to manufacture his presence. God has his own desire and will, and the Spirit expresses it by gifting and moving us (1 Corinthians 12:11), not by us manipulating him.

Third, the Spirit often speaks most clearly in the dark. We want to experience intimacy with God and clearly hear his voice, and I've found that we typically feel closest to him and hear him the loudest when we are in the darkest of places. Chan writes,

> From my own experience, I have felt closest to God when nearness to Him was a necessity. The Bible says that the Spirit comes through in situations where we would normally be afraid (Luke 12:11–12). We experience the Holy Spirit guiding us in desperate situations, such as being placed on trial for the gospel (in some countries), when we are asked why we believe in a God that allows _____ (fill in the

world's most recent tragic horror) to happen, or when we receive a totally unexpected phone call that a close family member has died.[2]

It's in the dark that the light of the Spirit shines the brightest. And it may be cliché to say, but I've heard the Spirit's voice more in those times of desperation. The Spirit gives us words when we need them to bear witness (Mark 13:11). He is the Helper and Comforter who goes with us when it seems like everything is against us.

> It's in the dark that the light of the Spirit shines the brightest. And it may be cliché to say, but I've heard the Spirit's voice more in those times of desperation.

Fourth, we must walk with the Spirit to know his voice. I bet you have friends whose voice you immediately recognize. Remember the days before caller ID when your phone rang and the person calling was a mystery? Someone might call, and you would answer, and she'd say, "Hey," and then start talking, but you still had no idea who it was. You'd be playing detective, trying to use what she was saying as clues to figure out who she might be. But you had other friends you knew just from the "Hey." You just knew their voice that well. You recognized their voice because your relationship was close, and you spent lots of time with them.

In the book of Ephesians, Paul tells us, "When you believed, you were marked in him [Christ] with a seal, the promised Holy Spirit, who is a deposit guaranteeing our

2. Chan, *Forgotten God*, 106–107.

inheritance" (Ephesians 1:13–14). Every born-again Christian is united to Christ, and our salvation can't be taken away from us. But our fellowship or walk with the Spirit isn't always as steady.

It's like a typical human friendship. There are people who will be our friends for a lifetime, but if we don't hang out—if we're not spending time with them—then the relationship suffers. Our relationship with God is the same way. When we're living in step with the Spirit, we're filled with his love, joy, and peace (see Galatians 5:22–23). But when we're disobedient to God, we can grieve the Holy Spirit (see Isaiah 63:10; Ephesians 4:30). You can walk out of step with the Spirit for a long time, and then you need to get on your knees and come back to him again. Communion is broken when we drift from or disobey our heavenly Father, but when we repent, rest our faith in Christ instead of ourselves, obey him, and spend time in the Word and prayer, we can experience the sweetness of his presence again.

I like to say that to hear the voice and promptings of the Spirit, you've got to know the Spirit. You can't listen to the Holy Spirit if you don't first know Jesus. And you won't hear his voice if you don't recognize it from spending time with his Word. For me, this involves learning to quiet my soul; I can't hear the Spirit if my life is too loud.

The amazing thing is that God wants to have a vibrant relationship with you. He wants you to walk and talk with him. And the more you read God's Word, the more he'll speak to you. Yes, he speaks through the Bible, but having heard his voice in the Word will help you identify the Holy Spirit's quiet promptings in your heart as well.

Finally, the Spirit moves us to action. The Holy Spirit brings you to a place where you need to express your faith. The Spirit leads you to active obedience to God's commission, which requires making real adjustments in your life (see Matthew 28:18–20; Acts 13:2; 15:28; 2 Corinthians 3:17–18). The adjustment may be small—like staying or leaving a club—or it may be big—like moving your family across an ocean. But Spirit-empowered obedience almost always involves an adjustment. Walking with the Spirit is an active thing more than an emotional thing (even if sometimes it does bring your emotions along).

Once you begin to listen to and obey the Spirit's voice, you're more prone to keep responding in obedience, because God proves himself faithful over and over. If he speaks to you and you don't listen, that doesn't mean he's never going to speak to you again. But if he speaks and you obey, you experience him in a deeper way. You get to see the fruit of obedience.

> **Once you begin to listen to and obey the Spirit's voice, you're more prone to keep responding in obedience, because God proves himself faithful over and over.**

That's my testimony. The Spirit spoke, I followed, and I experienced God in a way I never imagined. And then the next time he spoke, I experienced him even more.

Have you heard the Spirit's voice? If you haven't, then ask him to speak to you. Quiet your soul, open your eyes, and listen. The Holy Spirit's voice is discerned differently by each person, but his voice is almost always clear.

If you have heard the Spirit, have you obeyed? I don't know exactly what he's said to you, but I do know he's inviting you to go on a mission of bringing God's lost children home to him. Will you join him?

The Spirit's Song Moves the Mission Forward

It seemed like a normal Thursday at the little club. But that night was one I'll never forget. Joy was back in the dressing room again, leaning up against the makeup bar, crying. That was normal. She often lamented about how stuck she felt. And that night was the same except that the tears turned into a melody.

Amid her tears, Joy looked up and asked, "Can we sing a song?"

"I'd love to hear you sing," I told her.

She said, "Okay, I'll sing 'Amazing Grace.'"

We've all heard people sing "Amazing Grace," but I've never heard anyone sing it like Joy. Her voice was so powerful and beautiful it took my breath away. As Joy was singing, women started coming into the dressing room to listen. I'm still surprised the manager didn't run back there and put a stop to it.

There she was—this broken and desperate woman singing about how Jesus "saved a wretch like me." You could tell she meant what she was singing. Someone needed to pinch me. Was this really happening? Tears streamed down my cheeks as I felt God's holy presence. It was an emotional experience, but nothing we conjured up.

I wish I could tell you we shared the gospel and thirty women got saved that night, but it wouldn't be true. No, what happened is that for one small moment we got a glimpse of what the Holy Spirit was at work doing in one woman's soul.

And that moment was part of the journey that led Joy to recommit her life to the Lord and leave the lifestyle of dancing in the clubs behind.

God can do the craziest, most outrageously amazing things! There was a short time when we lost touch with Joy. But she came back into our lives about two years ago. Today, Joy is a beautiful volunteer in our ministry, working at the front desk of our resource center and serving as a mentor for women in our jobs program. And in many ways, she is exactly as I remember her in the clubs. She smiles ear to ear and has so much joy and peace despite all she's been through. Joy has every reason to be bitter and angry about the abuse she suffered and where it led her, but she isn't. Why? She's full of the Spirit.

I am so grateful the Spirit led us to this beautiful daughter of the King, his child who was lost and now has been found. I wonder where and to whom the Spirit is leading you.

PART 3

AS YOU GO,
BE SALT AND LIGHT

11

Salty Christianity

Going to the Hardest Places
as a Preserving Force

Jesus told you to go.

Do you ever ask him *where* he wants you to go? If you do, he will speak to you through his Spirit. But would you listen?

Corrie ten Boom learned to listen to the Holy Spirit early in her life. Then, when she was in a concentration camp, all she had was his voice. When Corrie was finally released, the Spirit guided her in ministry and used her as salt and light all around the world. Corrie modeled what it looks like to be certain of your calling and reliant on the Spirit to move you every moment of every day. She relied on the Spirit to move people to fund her mission and even had to rely on the Spirit for where to find her meals.

At one point, Corrie was doing ministry work in Africa but was praying, always open to where Jesus wanted her to go. She tells the story:

> [O]ne day during my quiet time, I began to feel that God was telling me it was time to leave Africa.
>
> "Lord, where do You want us to go?" I asked.
>
> "Argentina," came the answer deep in my heart.
>
> *Argentina?* I had never been to Argentina. I could not speak a word of Spanish. In those days air travel was sometimes poor in Africa, and to fly across the Atlantic Ocean to Buenos Aires would be a trying ordeal. Yet as I sat before the Lord, the word *Argentina* became even stronger.
>
> "Yes, but . . ." I started to answer Him. Then I remembered that obedience never says, "Yes, but . . ." Rather, it always says, "Yes, Lord!"[1]

Corrie ten Boom wasn't unaware of the difficulties that come for those who follow Christ. As a Holocaust survivor who lost her sister in a concentration camp, she was keenly aware. But she put aside all the "Yes, but . . ." excuses and embraced outrageous obedience. Why? She wrote in her book *Tramp for the Lord*, "Obedience is easy when you know you are being guided by a God who never makes mistakes."[2]

I love that she says obedience is easy, but the reality is that it seems difficult in a harsh and corrupt world.

Why?

Part of it is that Jesus doesn't just tell us to go to a place; he calls us to go to the *people* in that place, and those people are often hurting and may seem more sinful than we are.

1. Corrie ten Boom, *Tramp for the Lord* (New York: Jove Books, 1978), 97.
2. Ten Boom, *Tramp for the Lord*, 97.

Why Don't We Move Toward the Hurting?

I'll be honest, seeing the needs of hurting people all around me and watching church after church and Christian after Christian pass them by is harder than setting foot inside a strip club. I'm not saying I have all the answers or that I'm better than any other person. It's just heartbreaking to know the world is filled with people who have immense hurt and pain when Christians often turn their heads and walk the other way. Shouldn't being recipients of God's saving grace compel us to move toward hurting people, offering them that same grace?

Look at the books published for Christian women today. So many are focused on self. You know the messages they're giving you: Find your truth. Discover yourself. Clean yourself up. Girl, wash your . . . Well, you know. They're all about self-care, self-help, and self-improvement. They're turned inward toward *you.* Where are the books about keeping your eyes on Jesus, serving others without expecting anything in return, and following our Savior into the dark?

When I open my Bible, I don't see anything about who has the cutest Pinterest board or the most dynamic Instagram posts. Jesus looked at the most impressive, put-together people in his time and saw right through their facade to the darkness within. He didn't hold back when he told them, "You are like whitewashed tombs, which look beautiful on the outside but on the inside are full of the bones of the dead and everything unclean" (Matthew 23:27).

Now if this was just a problem with Christian publishing, that would be one thing, but the truth is that too often we also perpetuate a mission-stagnant, self-centered mentality in our churches. I mean, how many women's Bible studies have you been a part of? And how many of them motivated you to *GO*?

Jesus looked at the most impressive, put-together people in his time and saw right through their facade to the darkness within.

I believe fellowship and deep Bible study are great, but there's a problem when our fellowship groups and Bible studies keep us inside the church walls. It's wrong to merely gain a whole bunch of knowledge that doesn't move you. A deep walk with the Lord and knowledge of his Word should send us forward on mission. Depth of study should propel us into action.

We can be in countless Bible studies, and I personally have led many, but if studying the Bible doesn't move us to action, we have missed the point. I've met women who are safe inside the walls of a church, studying the Bible year after year, who haven't taken their faith and put it in action.

There are a lot of Christians who would rather donate clothes than know the person who will wear them. So many would rather throw junk food out the window at a person begging than take the time to get to know them. And there are countless agencies working to increase awareness about sex trafficking, but very few people in those agencies know women being trafficked. That has always unnerved me. For many Christians, it's easier to talk about the problem than know the people experiencing the problem. As Shane Claiborne writes:

[U]ltimately our hope is . . . that people can feel and taste the goodness of God and to find the salvation in Jesus's love and sacrifice. Sometimes the biggest barrier to that . . . has been a Church that is numb to the poverty of the world or just sees our Christianity as a ticket into heaven while ignoring the hells of the world around us.[3]

At Scarlet Hope, we're constantly pushing against that posture. We tell people, "Come, serve, and get to know the women; they are amazing," or, "Attend our outreach training and come to the clubs with us." Sadly, a lot of people react and say, "I just couldn't do that; I couldn't get that close to people like that!"

That is so sad.

Salty, Faith-Filled Obedience

Jesus told his followers, "You are the salt of the earth" (Matthew 5:13). Salt was used for lots of purposes in Jesus's day (just like in ours), but he most likely had in mind its power as a preservative. Jesus didn't want his followers to isolate themselves from other people; he wanted them to positively impact the world.

It's as if Jesus is saying, "You *are* the salt! In a corrupting world, you are to go where I send you and be a model of what it looks like to be a disciple. You are to be a preserving presence that shows the world what it means to follow me. Your outrageous obedience is intended to keep my world fresh and give it flavor." But, sadly, the gospel has been watered down in our culture for so long that the salt can't even be tasted.

3. Shane Claiborne, "Quotable Quote," (November 21, 2019), https://www .goodreads.com/quotes/455649-now-i-think-ultimately-our-hope-is-certainly -that-people.

Our faith must go beyond our Facebook posts. The way we live our lives needs to reflect the living God. We are called to preserve the gospel in the world by living salty, faith-filled lives that swim hard against the cultural currents that flow contrary to our faith.

> **Our faith must go beyond our Facebook posts. The way we live our lives needs to reflect the living God.**

What does it look like to be the salt of the earth?

First, being salt means resisting compromise. When you decide to live as a follower of Jesus, it's like jumping onto the first step of the "down" escalator, but you are walking up. In so many ways, culture is going in the wrong direction and trying to take you with it. Honestly, even our own selfish desires want to take us in the wrong direction. To follow Jesus, you will have to take deliberate steps to go in the opposite direction of everyone else and your own selfishness. The problem worsens because too often you will find other Christians going in the same (wrong and selfish) direction as culture instead of following Jesus. So as you take Spirit-guided steps, you're going to bump up against and need to push past Christians who are complaining, "What are you doing? We're going down, just turn around and come with us."

If you are trying to live a life of outrageous obedience, if you're committed to Jesus's command to go, I bet you've experienced that frustration more times than you can count.

At Scarlet Hope, we have had opportunities to remove Jesus from our mission. Why would we do that? We could get more funding. A *lot* more funding. But doing so would make us a social service agency rather than a ministry. Following Christ's call for our ministry means affirming the truth of God's Word and salvation through the grace, mercy, and redemption of Jesus Christ even if it means operating with less. Being salt means going against the grain of other nonprofits because we are concerned not only with women's physical state in this world but with their soul's state in the eternal life to come.

At Scarlet Hope, we love giving to those in need, but we don't measure our success based on how many meals we served or coats we passed out in the last month. Instead, we measure the number of women who have heard the gospel and how many are participating in our discipleship programs. There is a place for providing for a person's physical needs. But as Christians, we can't only operate clothes closets and soup kitchens, we must proclaim the gospel to the poor as well.

Where are *you* tempted to compromise?

- Scarlet Hope has been told we would be far more successful if we would just take Jesus out of what we do. Perhaps you're tempted to take Jesus out of your conversations with neighbors and coworkers.
- We know we would have more money if we left Jesus out of our ministry. You may realize you will probably make more money if you leave Jesus out of your workplace.

Where is it easy for you to go with everyone else down the escalator?

- In being obsessed with your appearance, home, or children's success in extracurricular activities?

- In finding acceptable what God says is unacceptable?
- In not going, like so many other Christians, even though Jesus told you to go?
- In not moving toward the hurting?

Second, being salt means engaging real needs and real people. You can find her at the entrance of one of the big malls. She's there begging—morning, noon, and night. I've given her money and food. On a few occasions, I've taken time to talk with her.

I've asked, "How are you? How are you feeling? How long have you been out here?" She's usually quiet and ashamed. The first time I spoke with her, I learned her name—Kelly—but she didn't say much more. On later visits, I learned Kelly is addicted to cocaine and heroin. That's what keeps her on the streets. When I heard that, I gave her my name and number on an index card and told her I'd come pick her up to take her to rehab. But she's not interested; she just stays at the mall. Kelly has diabetes—probably from all the Twinkies and other junk food people toss her way—and she's now lost one of her legs.

Sadly, Kelly has rejected many of the lifeboats God has sent her over the years. But I wonder if there might be increased motivation to change if more people who give her handouts also took time to build a relationship with her.

Is it so outrageous to think we might get to know hurting and broken people instead of judging and condemning them, or thinking they're not worth our time? If we did, would we have as many people standing on street corners? Would there be as many women having abortions? Would there be so many women looking for jobs in the clubs because they have five kids to feed and no money? I know Christ said the poor will always be among us (see Matthew 26:11), but he also told us that when we provide shelter, good food, and our presence to someone in need, it's like we're welcoming him (Matthew 25:31–46).

Though our focus is sharing the gospel, when someone is in need, you can't just give them a sympathetic look and an "I'll pray for you." If we're honest, we're tempted to say that a lot, but failing to address real needs can cut you off from relationship building. The truth is that it's meeting people's physical needs that provides the opportunity to meet their discipleship needs.

Now, I realize you may think, *I don't have time to do that.* I get it, and honestly, sometimes when I hear about people's messy, painful needs, I'm tempted to give the handout version instead of diving into a deeper conversation or relationship. But I need to tell you something. It has *never* been a bad decision, no matter the cost, to stop whatever I'm doing to love and serve a person with the love of Christ.

> **Who has God put in your life—a friend, relative, coworker—who is hurting and who you could move toward with love and compassion?**

I wonder: Who has God put in your life—a friend, relative, coworker—who is hurting and who you could move toward with love and compassion?

I also wonder: Who will God put in your path—a homeless person, a single mom struggling with her kids at the grocery store, someone sitting by herself crying at Starbucks? And will you seek to meet that person's need? Might you be able to use that opportunity to graciously talk to that person about the need they have for Jesus?

Finally, being salt means being humbly aware of our own brokenness and darkness. I think our biggest issue may be that we don't recognize our own sin, which makes us feel superior to others, especially others who don't have Jesus. That spirit of feeling better-than keeps us from moving toward the broken. Instead, we become unapproachable and judgmental.

Which is exactly the opposite of Jesus. Jesus may have been the most approachable person ever. People like lepers and prostitutes—who were actively shunned by society— felt free to approach Jesus.

Jesus was the most approachable and *least* judgmental person ever. The Bible says if you're guilty of sin, you can't judge the sin of others. That means we have no right to judge. But Jesus had no sin, so he *did* have the right to judge. Yet he didn't. Like the time when Jesus was presented with a woman who had been caught in the act of adultery and was about to be stoned to death. Jesus essentially said, "If you have no sin, you can judge her. You can give her what she deserves." And all her accusers dropped their stones and walked away, because they realized they were guilty of sin. But Jesus wasn't! So he could judge her. Yet he didn't. He said, "Neither do I condemn you. . . . Go now and leave your life of sin" (John 8:11).

The Pharisees acted like they were perfect. Jesus said that instead of helping people to experience life with God, they were slamming the door of heaven in people's faces and not allowing them to enter (see Matthew 23:13). How? By pretending they were perfect and by being unapproachable and judgmental. When we don't recognize our own sin, it leads us to be more like the Pharisees than we are like the one we claim to follow.

If the message of the gospel is true, we don't need white-washed, glow-up, Insta-worthy Christianity. We can and *must* be honest about our own sin and failures. Only then can we bask in the beautiful reality that God loves us and has chosen us even though he sees us in our least put-together moments. When we stop running and performing long enough to experience the reality of his love, it will compel us to love him more and move toward others with salty compassion.

From Difficulty to Joy

I can't lie to you. Corrie ten Boom said obedience is easy, but a lot of factors can make it hard. I see it all the time.

Earlier in the book, I mentioned the "next-shiny-object syndrome." Young women watch a Scarlet Hope promo video or read about our ministry and reach out to us. They say, "That's so powerful. I got chills." They're excited and ask, "How can I get involved?" But when we give them the next steps, all we hear are crickets.

I think these women were stirred not just by compelling stories but by the Holy Spirit. He prompted their hearts to obey. These women felt conviction, but then life got in the way of their following through. It's like the parable of the sower. Just as God's Word began to take root, the sun came out to scorch, weeds grew up to choke, and the enemy came to snatch away.

When we face the difficulties of obedience it's tempting to make excuses. I've heard them all:

> Wait a minute. You didn't mention in the video that we stay at the clubs until one in the morning. I've got to be up early. I'll be too tired.
>
> So you're telling me that when I share the gospel, some women will be hostile. A dancer might cuss me out or never talk to me again. That's not cool. I don't think this is for me.

The truth is that relational ministry is always difficult. It's not a good deed you can quickly mark off your spiritual checklist. It's hard. Relationships with broken people are messy. And, honestly, the response from Christians can be messy too. As Claiborne says,

> When people begin moving beyond charity and toward justice and solidarity with the poor and oppressed, as Jesus did, they get in trouble. Once we are actually friends with folks in struggle, we start to ask why people are poor, which is never as popular as giving to charity. One of my friends has a shirt marked with the words of late Catholic bishop Dom Helder Camara: "When I fed the hungry, they called me a saint. When I asked why people are hungry, they called me a communist." Charity wins awards and applause, but joining the poor gets you killed. People do not get crucified for charity. People are crucified for living out a love that disrupts the social order, that calls forth a new world. People are not crucified for helping poor people. People are crucified for joining them.[4]

4. Claiborne, *The Irresistible Revolution*, 129.

Just before Jesus told his followers "You are the salt of the earth," he spoke to them about persecution. He told them, "Blessed are you when people insult you, persecute you and falsely say all kinds of evil against you because of me. Rejoice and be glad, because great is your reward in heaven, for in the same way they persecuted the prophets who were before you" (Matthew 5:11–12).

Reno is a difficult city. It's different from Louisville in that the adult entertainment industry is out in the open; it's a fixture of the city. As a result, it's even more difficult to get Christians on board with the work there, because believers are no longer shocked or bothered by the strip clubs.

The director of our Scarlet Hope ministry in Reno has a line she repeats. When she meets with pastors or Christian leaders who aren't interested in partnering, she drops her classic line, "Okay, I'm going to do the work without you then." If you choose to obey Jesus, you may find yourself struggling to go up the down escalator *alone*.

What Motivates Salty Christianity?

When we move forward in obedience with God, toward difficult people and places, there will sometimes be disappointments, hardships, and perhaps even persecution. So what moves us to persevere in our obedience?

We persevere in obedience because of the joy that comes from the Holy Spirit. We choose whether we walk close with—and experience the fruit of—the Spirit or grieve him by our disobedience. The Spirit speaks to those who will obey. (Because he knows they will listen. Who wants to talk to someone who will tune out and ignore them?) When you are obedient, you get to experience the Spirit's life and presence. That experience motivates you to continue seeking, finding, and following him. As you join his work, you get to share in his joy and, someday, in the heavenly reward.

We also persevere in obedience because of the example of Jesus. The real heart of joyful, gritty obedience is recognizing that Jesus Christ obeyed for you. I said it frustrates me when Christians don't step out and live up to their calling. Jesus gets angry with complacent Christianity too. But Jesus went a step further. He went to the cross and became "obedient to death" (Philippians 2:8), absorbing the Father's wrath against our disobedience and sin. In love, he took the punishment of death and hell for our failure to obey.

So, yes, it is true that it's not always easy to obey, but we can because of Jesus's example and the joy of the Spirit. And Jesus gives us more than his example; he gives us his Holy Spirit. And the Spirit gives us more than joy; he gives us resurrection power so we *can* obey. Because we *need* to obey.

Make no mistake—we don't earn our salvation through obedience. We don't obey to be saved; we obey *because* we're saved. And we go into a dark and spoiled world, empowered to be salt and light by the Holy Spirit so *other people* can be saved.

Remember how Corrie ten Boom felt God was leading her to Argentina? Even though it made no sense, she said, "Yes, Lord," instead of, "Yes, but . . ."

After the spirit prompted her, Corrie reached out to a contact in Argentina, looking for opportunities to speak in churches and Christian ministries there. Though she didn't get a response from her contact, Corrie was so confident in the Spirit's call that she boarded a plane to South America.

When Corrie arrived in Argentina, she found out the contact had written to tell her he'd been unable to arrange any speaking engagements. He had told her not to come. Yet once Corrie was there, the Lord provided opportunity after opportunity for her to do ministry. She obeyed and so became a faith-filled, salty presence in Argentina. "What a joy I would have missed had I disobeyed," she wrote.[5]

You see, no matter the hardship, obedience is easy—well, maybe not easy, but definitely doable—when you are being guided by a God who never makes mistakes. And there is joy in obedience, because God is doing a preserving work in the world through those who are willing to outrageously obey.

5. Ten Boom, *Tramp for the Lord*, 100.

12

Bright Lights in Dark Spaces

Learning to Shine in the Hardest Situations

She blew out the fifty candles on her birthday cake. Ava was a victim of trafficking in her early teen years. We got to know her in a club and learned her birthday was coming up. Like Agnes—remember the Hawaiian prostitute in Tony Campolo's story—she had never had a birthday party. It was Agnes's story that sparked the idea to celebrate Ava's birthday in the club that night. It was a real-life opportunity to show the love of Christ to someone who felt so undeserving. She wasn't expecting it, and when we came in with a cake, she began to weep. The cake read "Happy Birthday Ava," and we gave her a gift, and everyone sang as loud as they could.

Ava thanked everyone and then, with tears in her eyes, pulled me aside and asked me to pray with her. After we finished praying, she said, "I have read this little Gideon Bible my whole life, and I've trusted that one day God would rescue me. Today as I blew out my birthday candles, I realized the greatest gift he has given me is rescuing me from the darkness by sending you church ladies into the club." That night, Ava packed up her belongings and walked out of the club for the last time. God brought her from darkness to light.

That's what we're supposed to do. We are the light of the world, and we are to shine Jesus's light so people won't have to live in darkness anymore.

A few years back, I took a trip to Israel and went to the Mount of Beatitudes, where tradition tells us Jesus delivered the Sermon on the Mount. The mount's slope sits off the northwest shore of the Sea of Galilee between Capernaum and Gennesaret.

What I remember most clearly about being there was the physical terrain. From that hillside, you can look across the sea and see the whole valley stretch out for miles on end. In other areas of Israel, our tour group would be corralled into little spaces and surrounded by trees. But here, the hillside was bare and cone-shaped like an amphitheater with an amazing vista behind it. You could see literally everything.

I remember thinking, *People stood here and listened to God himself preach a sermon!* It was on that hillside that Jesus said,

> You are the salt of the earth. But if the salt loses its saltiness, how can it be made salty again? It is no longer good for anything, except to be thrown out and trampled underfoot.

> You are the light of the world. A town built on a hill cannot be hidden.
>
> Matthew 5:13–14

From that spot on the slope overlooking the sea, you could see how important the towns up on the hillsides were. If it was dark and stormy, they'd be like lighthouses up above the water, guiding fishermen safely home. "In the same way," Jesus said, "let your light shine before others, that they may see your good deeds and glorify your Father in heaven" (Matthew 5:16).

There's no point going into the darkness if you don't have the light of Christ in you. That would be like the blind leading the blind. The reason missionaries cross oceans, the reason Christians set up pregnancy centers, and the reason we go into the strip clubs is so that those who are lost in the dark might come to see the glory and the light of Christ.

The reason missionaries cross oceans, the reason Christians set up pregnancy centers, and the reason we go into the strip clubs is so that those who are lost in the dark might come to see the glory and the light of Christ.

The Man in the VIP Booth

Our team used to minister in a small club called The Diamond, where there were VIP booths in which men could sit in the dark. The owner of the club sat there among those men. We knew he was there, but we could never see him. Honestly, the VIP booths were never really an area we focused on. Our team of ladies would go straight to the back of the club or to the side of the stage where we sometimes set up our tables.

One day, after we'd been ministering in this club for a year, I walked in and saw this slight man in his late seventies who was wearing a suit. He was sitting at the bar as I came in. As soon as I saw his physical presence, I knew he was the owner.

He stopped me and asked, "Are you in charge of this, all this stuff?"

"Yeah," I answered with a smile. But inside I was thinking, *Oh my gosh, we're getting kicked out.*

"You know, I've never met you," he said, "but I'm the owner here, and I've been watching you church ladies for a year. . . . I have never seen such bright lights. I've never seen people who love other people like you've loved and served the dancers in my club."

I was taken aback. He'd watched us for a whole year?

I got to talk to him and share the gospel with him that night. I don't know what God ultimately did in his heart. I never saw him again, but he heard the good news, and I hope one day he responded and glorified God.

Thinking back, I realize I wouldn't have even had that chance to share the gospel if our team hadn't been a consistent light in that dark place. This owner saw the team's good deeds. He watched them come in and out every week, sitting with the dancers and caring for them. He saw their outrageous obedience.

Moving from Stuck to Outrageous Obedience

But what if the team had never gone? What if they never stepped out and stepped in? What if, like so many, they felt the dissonance between a comfortable Christian culture and a life truly lived on mission for God—but never experienced what it means to discern God's call and then follow him in outrageous obedience?

Maybe that's you.

Perhaps you identify with trauma, and you know how it feels to be judged and misunderstood. Though this is true, you've found Christ loves you despite your difficult past. Now you want to be a safe and courageous help to other vulnerable people in crisis, but you don't know where to start.

It could be you're a young Christian, and you're moved and compelled by the ministry stories you've read in this book. You want to take risks for Jesus, but you're not sure where to begin.

Or maybe you feel like you're too old for outrageous obedience. This book has been entertaining, but you're thinking, "I wish I had done that when I was in my twenties." You've put obedience to a ministry call on hold so often—while you raised your children, while you pursued a career, while you managed a hectic life. Now you've come to the end of the book and you're wondering if it's just too late for you.

If you've been reading along but still feel stuck, I want to take a few pages before I bring the book to a close to make all this as practical as possible. Here are seven steps to help you move toward active obedience.

First, identify where you feel stuck, and confess the reasons to God. Think about what has kept you from obedience. What has you running from God and his mission for you? Is it fear? Comfort? A judgmental attitude? An inability to be still and simply hear his voice? The first step toward outrageous obedience is being honest about the behaviors and attitudes that have kept you from obeying in the first place. Identify those obstacles and repent of them. Confess your sin to the Lord and remember that he is faithful to forgive (1 John 1:9).

Second, remember God's faithfulness. Call to mind his promises. Think about the times when he has done exactly what he says he'll do. You may not have experienced a physical healing like I did as a child, but I'm certain there have been times when God has shown up for you. Remember those moments. Remember how God has been faithful to keep his promises, how he was there in your desperation, how he stayed true even when your faith wavered. Claim the truth that he's still faithful even if you've been letting obstacles keep you from obedience. His name is Faithful and True, so draw near to him.

Third, spend time with Jesus. Open God's Word. And don't just study the Bible for information; read the Bible for transformation. Don't just read to master the content; read to know the Master. Make sure that when you're spending time in God's Word, you're spending time in communion with God. As you open your Bible, ask the Holy Spirit to speak to you through the Word. Ask him to show you how the Savior meets you in your great need. Read through the Word slowly—verse by verse and paragraph by paragraph—until you sense what the Spirit behind the words (and never contrary to the words) is saying to you. Then, write down what he's said. As you learn to discern the Spirit's voice in his Word, you'll be more apt to hear his voice throughout your life. That brings us to the next practical step toward obedience.

Fourth, recognize where God is working around you. Remember, God loves you in a real and personal way, so you can count on the fact that he wants to involve you in his work. You don't have to manufacture a ministry or concoct a calling. God is inviting you to join him. He will speak to you—through his Word, through his people, through his Spirit, and through your circumstances—to call you to join him where he's already working in the world.

Where do you see him working in your circumstances and relationships? Where is the Spirit already moving your heart? Is there a people or place for which God has given you a burden? Are you overflowing with compassion as Jesus was when he saw the city and wept over it (Luke 19:41)? Is there someone in your life who you can look toward and love despite their brokenness—the way Jesus saw and loved the rich young ruler (Mark 10:21)? Is there a sinner or a broken place to which God is turning your head with compassion and tears of love? If you've noticed God working in your church or city, or if God has given you a burden—whether it be for a particular part of the world or a sector of society—don't suppress those promptings. Your observations and burdens may be what the Spirit is using to call you to outrageous obedience. It could be that he's opening your heart to a new work.

> Don't suppress those promptings. Your observations and burdens may be what the Spirit is using to call you to outrageous obedience.

Fifth, ask others to pray with you. Find a group of friends and share with them what you've noticed about how God is moving. Share your passion with them. Scarlet Hope would never have started without those months driving around town in my little Ford Focus, praying. We would have never entered the Fantasy X strip club without first praying over it at the Wendy's across the street. I would never have moved forward to start the ministry without Josh cheering me on. Often God uses other people to confirm our calling and encourage us in it. So don't keep what you're hearing from the Holy Spirit to yourself. Bring others along and let your communion with God overflow into communion with others.

Sixth, do some research. When Scarlet Hope began, we first did our homework. Our group of ladies attended the trafficking workshop in Lexington, and I spent days researching the adult entertainment industry on my computer at work and talking to other people. Now we require everyone who volunteers to attend a mandatory orientation where we review what serving in the clubs involves. Most service and mission organizations take that same approach. As you consider what outrageous obedience is going to look like for you, take some time to count the cost and learn exactly what it's going to take (Luke 14:28). It's only then that you'll be ready for the final step.

Finally, get up and go! Following God's call will mean making some adjustments in your life. You'll have to put obedience on your calendar. You might even have to hire a babysitter. Just as it did with Esther, God's invitation for us to work with him always involves a concrete crisis of belief that requires putting our faith into action. It will require the courage to move past your fear and love of comfort. You might even need to make major adjustments in your life to join God in what he is doing. Like Corrie ten Boom, you might have to board a plane and move to a different part of the country or a different part of the world. But obeying God is always worth it. Risk-taking, adjustment-making faith that moves a bright light into the dark is a pathway to joy.

Letting Your Light Shine Is Always Worth It

At the beginning of the journey God called me to, I can remember a moment where I asked myself, *Are you willing to take this risk?* Everyone was telling me how dangerous the adult entertainment industry is, and I remember having a conversation with Josh where we talked about the violence that sometimes erupts in the clubs. I had to ask, *Am I willing to risk my life?*

Whenever those questions would arise, I'd think about Esther. She was willing. She went in before the king for the good of her people. She had to walk out on faith. And who was she trusting in that moment? Was it simply Mordecai? Was she just trusting that what he said would work? Maybe a little. But it's clear she also was trusting God both to deliver her people and to deliver her.

Recently we began a new Scarlet Hope ministry down in Miami, Florida. We gathered a group of women to go into the first club, and I remember a woman—we'll call her Laura—sitting in the back seat of our car as we drove up to the club. I looked back and said, "Are you okay, Laura?"

"I'm having a panic attack," she answered. "But you're still here after fourteen years. God has been faithful to you; I guess I can trust that he'll be faithful to me too."

That's my prayer for you as you close this book. Not that you'll see my ministry at Scarlet Hope but that you'll hear of God's faithfulness to me, and that it will inspire you to obey him no matter how overwhelmed or panicked you feel. No matter who says you can't. No matter what you must give up . . . *You. Can. GO.* Because our faithful God goes with you, you can be a light where it's dark, and you can experience the joy of outrageous obedience.

ACKNOWLEDGMENTS

I want to acknowledge Jesus as my Lord and Savior. Without him first and foremost in my life I would not be the woman he has created me to be. I'm eternally grateful to the Lord for calling me to his glorious kingdom work at such a young age. I count it a privilege to get to partake in this work each day. I also want to thank the countless people who have believed in the mission and work of Scarlet Hope, who have believed in the gospel advancing in the adult entertainment industry, and who have showered this ministry with kindness.

People come and go throughout life, but there are many who have made a lasting impact on my life and made this book possible. Ruth Schenk was captured by the heart of our ministry so many years ago, and she has never stopped believing that there was a story to be written that would inspire many others.

Sarah Flannery, thank you for believing in the vision God had given to me, and thank you for being willing to outrageously obey the Lord by going with me into the darkness. Because of your friendship and help getting this ministry started, thousands of women have been freed. Thank you, sister, for your trust in me as a leader to do something outrageous for the Lord.

Emily Williams dedicated her life to working alongside me in the ministry. Thank you for being there and encouraging me every step of the way. Like Ruth and Naomi, we will go to the end together.

I am forever grateful for the friendship and leadership of Ronelle Brumleve, who has devoted her life's work to reaching women with the gospel. Without your trust and care of Scarlet Hope Louisville, the ministry would not be advancing to other areas where women are in darkness. You are a light to many, and I thank the Lord for you.

I want to thank all of the Scarlet Hope volunteers who have served in ways that have been significant. You have made a lasting impact on many lives. Kate Blanchard, Lori Riggs, and Monica Deskin, I'm so grateful for your unwavering support for over a decade. You are outrageously obedient, and I thank the Lord for each of you.

And without donations to care well for the lives of the women God has put in our path, we would not have been able to accomplish all that God laid out for us. I am grateful for Denise Clements, who showed up at the Hope House with curtains and who answered the call to disciple and walk alongside me all these years. Thank you to Len Moisan, Dave Stone, Anna Bates, and Brian Howard for coaching me and opening doors that the Lord has used to accomplish his work.

Thanks to all the board members who have led with integrity and grit. You have challenged me to be a better leader every step of the way.

I am especially grateful to my agent and former Scarlet Hope board member, Don Gates, for supporting the ministry, encouraging me as a leader, and working together with our ministry to advance the gospel in ways—like this book—that I could never have imagined. Thank you for believing there was a book inside me. Without your dedication, we would not be here.

Thank you to my editor, Jared Kennedy, for the countless hours, thought, and dedication you have put into making this not just a good book, but a great book. I am forever grateful for your pushing me to the end. This book would not have been possible without your support and kindness to me throughout this process.

Through an unlikely string of events, Vince Antonucci, you have been a gift to the impact of this book and my own life. I have learned much, and I know that through your weaving of words, you have helped craft this into a much better book. Thank you for your tireless work to see this book through.

Thanks to the team at Bethany House Publishers for believing in me and trusting me as an author. I'm so grateful for your work in editing, producing, and marketing this book as well. Thank you for helping me push God's call to obedience out into the world.

My life has forever been impacted by thousands of women who have shown up in these pages (with names changed to protect their identities) as a testimony of how God's light shines into one of the darkest areas of our society. The God of hope has come to redeem and restore every woman he has called according to his purpose.

And last, but most important, thank you to my parents and to my husband. Mom and Dad, thank you for raising me to know Jesus. Thank you for caring for me through the years of medical hardship. Thank you for showing me what it meant to live and love as Jesus does. I am eternally grateful to you, my parents, and I thank God for your being my first examples of outrageous obedience. I love you.

Finally, and most of all, I cannot thank my beloved husband, Joshua, enough for believing in the work of this ministry and the calling Jesus gave me, and for the dedication and support to faithfully love me every step of the way.

Rachelle Starr founded Scarlet Hope, a nonprofit dedicated to sharing the hope of Jesus with women in the adult entertainment industry. Rachelle also leads a gospel-centered career development program where women can receive employment and job skills while discovering their God-given gifts and talents. Rachelle and her husband, Josh, have two boys and reside in Louisville, Kentucky. Learn more at scarlethope.org and by following @rachellestarr.co on Instagram.